The Dynamics of
Church
Leadership

Other books in the
Ministry Dynamics for a New Century series
WARREN W. WIERSBE, series editor

The Dynamics of
Church
Leadership

AUBREY MALPHURS

Baker Books

A Division of Baker Book House Co
Grand Rapids, Michigan 49516

Published by Baker Books
a division of Baker Book House Company
P.O. Box 6287, Grand Rapids, MI 49516-6287

Printed in the United States of America

Library of Congress Cataloging-in-Publication Data

Malphurs, Aubrey.
    The dynamics of church leadership / Aubrey Malphurs
        p.   cm. — (Ministry dynamics for a new century)
    Includes bibliographical references and index.
    ISBN 0-8010-9090-3 (pbk.)
    1. Clergy—Office. 2. Christian leadership. 3. Pastoral theology.
  I. Title II. Series
  BV660.2.M23   1999
  253—dc21   99–38440

For current information about all releases from Baker Book House, visit our web site:
                    http://www.bakerbooks.com

Contents

97662

Series Preface

The purpose of the Ministry Dynamics series is to provide both experienced and beginning pastors with concise information that will help them do the task of ministry with efficiency, fruitfulness, and joy.

The word *ministry* means "service," something that Jesus exemplified in his own life and that he expects us to practice in our lives. No matter what our title or position, we are in the church to serve God's people. The word *dynamics* is not used as an equivalent of "power" but as a reminder that nothing stands still in Christian ministry. If it does, it dies. True biblical ministry involves constant challenge and change, learning and growth, and how we handle these various elements determines the strength and success of the work that we do.

The emphasis in this series is on practical service founded on basic principles and not on passing fads. Some older ministers need to catch up with the present, while newer ministers need to catch up on the past. We all can learn much from each other if only we're honest enough to admit it and humble enough to accept each other's counsel.

I began pastoring in 1950 and over the years have seen many changes take place in local church ministry, from bus ministries and house churches to growth groups and megachurches. Some of the changes have been good and are now integrated into God's work in many churches. But some ideas that attracted national attention decades ago now exist only on the pages of forgotten books in used-book stores. How quickly today's exciting headlines become tomorrow's foot-notes! "Test everything. Hold on to the good" (1 Thess. 5:21).

An ancient anonymous prayer comes to mind:

From the cowardice that shrinks from new truth,
From the laziness that is content with half-truths,
From the arrogance that thinks it knows all truth,
   O God of truth, deliver us!

Our desire is that both the seasoned servant and the new seminary graduate will find encouragement and enlightenment from the Ministry Dynamics series.

Warren W. Wiersbe

Introduction

"According to the weather channel, it's around ten degrees outside, but this ought to warm you up some," Pastor Steve Morris said as he poured some hot coffee for Pastor Bob Smith. The two men were sitting in comfortable overstuffed chairs in Steve's spacious new church office. Steve, in his late forties and the more experienced pastor, had volunteered his time and expertise to mentor Bob, pastor of Grace Family Church.

"There's so much I would like to share with you," Steve continued. "I've learned a great deal over the past twenty years here at Northpoint Community Church. You'll have to let me know if what I outline today is more than you bargained for."

Pastor Bob shook his head. "I'm sure it won't be," he said. "I need all the help I can get." Bob was determined to make this fourth pastorate in nine years a success. He wanted to avoid the mistakes he had made in the three small churches he had previously pastored. When the opportunity had come for his small church to be paired for a year with the much larger Northpoint through a teaching church network, he and his membership had been excited by the possibilities. Pastor Steve was well known as a natural and gifted leader of a church that had in twenty years grown from 150 to 1,500 members through an unusually balanced combination of evangelism and transfer growth. Pastor Bob and his people knew they would benefit from the association with a man who had had an extraordinary impact on the community for Christ.

"I thought we'd begin," Steve said, "by getting to know each other and planning some of our meetings over the next year. Why don't you begin? Tell me about your life before coming to Grace."

"Well, nine years ago I graduated, with no pastoral experience, from seminary. The school emphasized academics, and most of my training took place in the classroom. Since then I have pastored three small, struggling churches, and it doesn't take a mathematical genius to figure out that at all three my tenure was short-lived. Now I'm in my first year at Grace and realize that I need someone to help me develop my leadership skills and capabilities as a pastor, and that's why I'm here."

Steve smiled and encouraged Bob to continue. "Tell me a little about Grace."

Bob began to relay facts about Grace that he had only recently learned himself. "Ten families planted Grace Family Church in the 1950s as a traditional, independent work that had pulled out of a denomination that the founders felt had gone liberal."

Steve sighed. "That's not the best way to start a church," he said.

"No it's not, but it worked for Grace, because it grew to over 450 people within its first ten years of existence. But after twenty years of fruitful ministry, the founding pastor left because of some problems with the board. Since his departure, the church has steadily declined to its present size of 100 to 120 mostly elderly people and has gone through eight pastors with an average of two to three years tenure, excluding the first who stayed four years."

"Whew!" Steve leaned forward. "That's not an encouraging situation!"

"No it's not," Bob agreed. "But I believe that God has called me to be a pastor, and I plan to hang in there until I die—or they run me off!"

The two men chuckled. Then Steve said, "You know, Bob, your situation isn't at all uncommon. You're not alone. Numerous pastors and churches across denominational lines all across North America find themselves in a similar situation. I would estimate that 70 to 80 percent of the churches in this area of the country are plateaued or in decline."

"That doesn't surprise me," Bob said. "I've begun meeting periodically and informally with a group of pastors, and most of them are ministering under the same or similar circumstances."

Bob paused and seemed to be studying the Northpoint logo on his coffee mug. When he began speaking again, he chose his words carefully. "I have to admit I frequently wrestle with discouragement and occasionally with bouts of depression, but my main concern is my family." Bob glanced at Steve and then looked away. "It's been particularly difficult for my wife, Jill. She worries about the impact that this church is having on our two kids. When they were younger, they were happy anywhere. Their needs were met in whatever Sunday school they were in. But now they're approaching adolescence, and Jill questions whether our church will be able to provide an adequate program for them as they mature. We have many wonderful older people who long to see our church reinvent and relive life as it was in the 1950s. They envision ministry the same way they did then. We don't have much of a youth program now, and the few teens we have seem to disappear into the woodwork when they graduate from high school. Jill fears that without a vibrant youth ministry, our kids could emotionally and spiritually walk away from the church and, in time, the faith. That's very frightening."

"It sure is," Steve agreed. "But I believe your leadership can bring your church into the new millennium in time to minister to the needs of your children."

"I sure hope so, Steve. I'm counting on you to help me do it."

Steve nodded thoughtfully, then got up to get the coffeepot. After refilling both mugs, Steve sat back down and said, "I have to ask you a difficult question. Are you sure that you belong in the ministry and that God has wired you to be a point pastor?"

"That's a fair question," Bob responded. "I have taken a spiritual gifts inventory and spent some time going through an assessment program. Because of the results of those and my experience, I have no doubts now that God has directed me into pastoral ministry."

"That's important," Steve said, "because if you had come to some other conclusion, we might not have a need to meet any further. And that would have been okay because the church of Jesus Christ needs godly laypeople as well as professionals.

"Okay, Bob, let's talk about what you see as your ministry strengths and weaknesses."

"Well, I love to preach and teach the Scriptures. Ever since I first came to faith on a college campus, I have had a thirst for studying and learning the Bible. As my knowledge grew, my college church invited me to speak on occasion in an adult Sunday school class. Eventually they asked me to become its teacher. I discovered that I'm a reasonably good communicator—at least that's what people tell me. I really enjoy standing in front of a group of people who are serious about their faith and want to learn more about the Bible. That turns me on!" Bob paused, waiting for Steve's response, but when Steve said nothing, Bob went on. "I believe that I have a gift of teaching and preaching. That's why I went to seminary—to develop these gifts and secure the needed credentials. The school did an excellent job of teaching me the Bible, the languages, theology, church history. And they trained me to preach. I'll always be grateful for that. Most of my training focused on preparing me for the one hour of preaching on Sunday morning. I'm realizing that they did little to prepare me for leadership and the problems I've faced in the churches I've pastored. They gave me the impression that pastoring a church was 95 percent preaching and teaching the Bible and 5 percent pastoral care. I liked that, but when I got into pastoral ministry I discovered, as my grandpa would say, 'that dog wouldn't hunt!'"

Steve laughed a wide-mouthed, hearty laugh. Then he grew quiet and serious again. "A few minutes ago, you indicated that you have no doubts that God has 'wired' you to be a pastor. That means you're probably a visionary."

"Yes," Bob responded, "not too long ago I took the *Kiersey Temperament Sorter* and scored high on the N or intuitive preference, which seems to be a characteristic of visionaries. My focus is more on what could be than what is. I spend much time dreaming big dreams as I envision where my church could be in a few years."

"And, you know," Steve said, "the taller and more expansive your dream, the deeper your foundation must be. The foundation is your personal integrity as a leader. That's one of the important topics we'll discuss as we meet together. Bob, I have carved out one to two hours in my schedule to meet with you every week. Will that work for you?"

"Yes! You don't know how much I appreciate this. I have tons of questions and look forward to our time together. I consider it a privilege to sit under your training. Pastors and laypeople in this community view you as a gifted, skilled man of integrity whom God is using to have an impact for Christ."

Steve blushed. "It won't take you long to see through all that! For the most part I have enjoyed pastoral ministry, and as it says of David in Acts 13:36, my desire is that God use me to serve his purpose in this generation. Much sweeping change is taking place not only in the world in general but the church in particular. Many new-paradigm churches are coming on the scene, and who knows what is on the horizon? I welcome most of these new churches. I find them to be a breath of much-needed ministry fresh air. Like you were saying about your church, far too many of our evangelical churches continue to operate on traditions forged in the nineteenth and early twentieth centuries in western Europe. At the same time, however, though I'm interested in and attempt to follow ministry trends, I'm not interested in the latest ministry fads that may be replaced by other, similar fads six months down the road. Neither am I locked into a 'one size or model fits all' philosophy. I don't for a moment believe that everything we do here at Northpoint is best for you. In fact I'm convinced it's not. Obviously we're much bigger than you and the ministry and leadership dynamics for us are different than they are for you at Grace. However, I'm convinced that you can learn from us and use some of the fundamental, essential principles that we and so many other churches have built on since the inception of the church in the first century."

Bob was nodding in agreement.

Steve continued, "What I desire is to cover some of the dynamics of pastoral ministry. I have given some thought to these and already outlined in my mind our first six meetings. After that, we can reevaluate our time together and the content of our discussions. Here are my thoughts." Steve moved a pad of paper to the center of the low table that was between them. On it he had written topics for each session:

Session 1: Godly character. How is godly character developed?
Session 2: Leadership.
Session 3: The work of the church.
Session 4: Relationship between pastor and people.
Session 5: Change. What is a theology of change?
Session 6: Culture. What is a theology of culture?

As he pointed to *godly character,* he said, "My biggest challenge in ministry has been to develop godly character. However, my greatest adversary in this, believe it or not, is the ministry itself! We need to talk about this." Then he pointed to *leadership.* "We'll need to discuss what leadership is; what pastors do as leaders; and how you know if you're a leader. In our third session, I want to explore with you what is going on in your church. I plan to ask you some hard questions."

"Such as?" Bob asked.

"Such as, What are you doing as a church, and What has Christ asked you to do? And once you're sure about what you're supposed to be doing, how will you do it? These are the core ministry questions that every church must ask and answer. Some of this will be easy and some positively 'gut wrenching.'"

Bob's raised eyebrows showed his surprise but he let Steve continue without interrupting.

"In our fourth session, I want to probe how you relate to your people—your congregation, any staff, and the board. The key to the effectiveness of a church ministry is its people. A church is only as good as the people who comprise it. Who are your people, and what are your responsibilities to them? How do you relate to one another? You intimated earlier that some problems might exist there. Next, we will look at change. We're going through a time of turbulent, chaotic change that this country has never experienced before. It's imperative that future pastors know how to deal with change. How should churches and their leaders respond to change? Have you developed a theology of change?" Steve pointed to the last topic. "Then we need to talk about culture. Is culture good or bad? Most believe that it's bad. I'll help you think about and begin to develop a theology of culture."

Bob felt overwhelmed as he began to glimpse how much he needed to learn. But he was also excited because he sensed that in Pastor Steve he had a capable mentor. He expressed his concern to Steve.

"Whatever efforts you make will be well worth it," Steve assured him. "God will be honored and your people blessed."

"That is what I'm praying for, Steve," Bob said.

In my consulting and training practice, I have met many point pastors whom God hasn't designed to be in that position. When they discover this, most seem very relieved because they've struggled in that role. I suggest that all people in professional ministry go through a good assessment program to make sure that who they are fits with what they are doing. I also recommend reading my book *Maximizing Your Effectiveness* (Grand Rapids: Baker, 1995). It helps in the assessment process.

Pastors and
Their Character

Knowing Who You Are

"I've been thinking all week about today's topic," Bob said as he sat down with Steve for their session on godly character.

"Really? What were you thinking?"

"Well, you said that the development of godly character is the greatest challenge of ministry but that the ministry itself is the greatest adversary of godly character. I've been trying to figure out what that means."

Steve smiled and reached for his Bible. "I hope it will become clear today. I sometimes refer to godly character as the sanctification of the soul. I believe it's the greatest challenge we face in life. I think that's why Paul puts so much emphasis on godliness in such passages as 1 Timothy 4:7–8." Steve read the following:

> Have nothing to do with godless myths and old wives' tales; rather, train yourself to be godly. For physical training is of some value, but godliness has value for all things, holding promise for both the present life and the life to come.

When Steve looked up from his reading, he said, "I want to tell you about my father-in-law. He was a retired pastor and one of the godliest men I know. He died recently of a heart attack."

"I'm sorry," Bob said. "That must have been hard on your family."

"Yes, it was." Steve paused, stretched, and then went on. "He was like a father to me and he was the primary person that God used in my life to encourage me to move toward pastoral ministry. I had plans to pursue a career in the corporate world, but he patiently pointed out how my gifts and temperament were perfectly suited to ministry—especially my communication and leadership gifts. He was so encouraging! It felt good simply to be around the man. And I found it difficult to resist his wisdom and council because of his character. He was for me what Paul writes in Galatians 4:19 when he talks about Christ being formed in us. That man embodied for me the fruit of the Spirit—the very character of Christ. I'm not sure that I would be in ministry today had it not been for him. I wanted to tell you about him because he's such a good example of our topic today."

Godly Character

"As you know, I'm convinced, after many years in ministry and working with other pastor friends, that the greatest challenge we face in life is developing godly character. And I'm convinced that people want, above all else, leaders of good character. They want to believe in their leaders; they want to have faith and confidence in them as people. They want assurance that their word is trustworthy and that they're excited and enthusiastic about the church's direction. Godly character is the foundation of that kind of leadership.

"However, and this is what puzzled you, I have also found that the greatest impediment to the goal of godly character is the ministry itself. I want to divide today's session into two parts. First, let's examine the conflict between ministry and character and why it is that ministry can impede one's character development. Then we can talk about what I think is the solution to this conflict: Understanding both character and the ministry and how they relate."

Bob was listening intently and jotting notes as Steve talked. "You know," he said, "this sounds like something I've been struggling with since I began my pastoral ministry—the constant battle to balance ministry achievement with character development."

The Conflict between Ministry and Character

"Yes, that's it," Steve agreed. "Here's the problem as I see it. According to such texts as Matthew 25:14–30; Romans 12:3–8; and 1 Corinthians 12, our wonderful God—based solely on his grace—has invested in us certain gifts, talents, and abilities. Then he invites us to use them to serve him and advance his kingdom here on earth. These God-given talents and gifts allow us to do some exciting and eternally significant things for God's kingdom, not the least of which is leading Christ's church. At the same time, our gifts and abilities coupled with our ministry accomplishments present us with both an opportunity and a temptation. On the one hand, the opportunity is to have maximum kingdom impact while here on earth. On the other hand, the temptation is to allow our hearts and souls to shrivel as our gifts and talents grow and accomplish much."

The Dark Night of the Soul

Steve leaned forward as he spoke. "For leaders to be effective, however, they must realize that their character development is as important as their ministry success. The problem is that far too many of us become lost in the shuffle and practice of ministry. We place excessive and unrealistic expectations on ourselves, and people demand much from us. It's not unusual to put in fourteen- to eighteen-hour days—especially if we love what we do. And eventually we find that our talents and abilities create for us opportunities to *do* that exceed our capacity to *be*."

Bob nodded in agreement. He had been there.

"The result," Steve continued, "is that all this, in time, leads to what I refer to as a 'dark night of the soul.' The distance between who we are and what we accomplish grows and the discrepancy between being and doing leads to pretending."

Bob looked up from his notes. "What do you mean?" he asked.

Steve explained, "We sense a great gap between our walk with Christ and our work for Christ, yet we pretend as the hymn says that all is well with our souls. We wear spiritual masks to hide what we suspect is our true condition. We are living in the danger zone of pretense, and the greater our success, the more time we spend alone in that carnal zone. We become remote and isolated, avoiding the people who may find us out. This hypocrisy leads to further emptiness on the inside that, if not caught and dealt with, eventually results in some type of disaster."

"I think I've seen that happen," Bob said.

The Ministry Toll

Steve nodded. "I'm sure you have. We can look back on the last two decades of the twentieth century in particular and see the wake of destruction that ministry hypocrisy has left in its path. Pastors as well as television evangelists have literally been caught with their pants down, their hands in the offering plates, and worse."

Bob would have smiled at Steve's words but the gravity of what he was saying was too real. Steve picked up the morning paper that was lying on the table. "Hardly a month goes by that we don't hear or read in the newspapers about some well-known pastor who has had an affair and left the ministry. What a terrible impact that must have on the man and on his family as well!"

Steve dropped the paper back on the table. "It seems that the church's most sacred and spiritual traditions have been violated. As a consequence of scandal, the people in our churches feel betrayed and violated and many become disillusioned. Far too many become cynical toward leadership and some join the ranks of the Christian unchurched. They pass through a 'dark night of the soul' themselves and come away empty. Those who aren't Christians and are unchurched use all this to justify being, and remaining, unchurched. They turn a cold, deaf ear to Christianity in general and the church in particular."

"This is scary," Bob said, leaning back and resting his elbows on the arms of his chair. "I feel like this could be me! What you've described is to some degree what

I've felt in the past and may be going through now. Often I put in fourteen- to eighteen-hour days trying to accomplish what needs to be done. I feel good about the gifts and abilities God has given me. But it's true that the time I put into the practice of my ministry far exceeds the time I put into the development of my character. I may be heading for that danger zone of pretension and the 'dark night of the soul.'"

Understanding Character and Ministry and How They Relate

"I speak from personal experience as well," Steve admitted. "I suspect that all of us in leadership go through this experience. The question isn't, Do we wear spiritual masks? The question is, What do we do when we find ourselves living a life of hypocrisy behind those masks? In short, what is the solution to this problem? I believe that the solution is a proper understanding of character and ministry and how the two relate. This involves working our way through six vital areas."

Steve handed Bob a sheet of paper on which had been typed the following chart:

	Character	Ministry
Essence	being (who I am)	doing (what I do)
Components (tools)	heart, soul, spirit	gifts, talents, skills
God's role	what God does *in us* (objects of his grace)	what God does *through us* (vehicles of his grace)
Our role	to be *with him*	to do *for him*
Relationship	first	second
Temptation	presumed	trained

The Essence of Character and Ministry

Steve pointed to the word *essence*. "As I said, the essence of character is being, whereas the essence of ministry is doing. Character involves who I am, while ministry involves what I do. The former reflects my capacity to be, and the latter reflects my capacity to do. God wants me to be a certain kind of person in him and he wants me to do kingdom work for him."

My Character

"So what kind of person does God want me to be?" Bob asked, feeling like he already knew the answer.

"He wants you, and me, to be like the Savior," Steve answered. "Look at Galatians 4:19. Paul writes, 'My dear children, for whom I am again in the pains of childbirth until Christ is formed in you.'"

Bob had been following along in his Bible. Now he looked up. "I have to admit, Steve, I'm not sure what it means to have 'Christ formed in you.'"

"For the longest time, I didn't know what that meant, either," Steve said. "But I think God has cleared this up for me. In John 14:17 Jesus promises before his death that in the future the Holy Spirit will come and be in the believer. After Jesus' death, Paul teaches in 1 Corinthians 6:19 that now the Holy Spirit indwells the Christian. Then in Ephesians 5:18 he commands us to be filled or controlled by the Spirit. Look at Galatians 5:16, 18, and 25. Here Paul commands believers to 'live,' be 'led by,' and 'keep in step' with the Spirit. The result of this relationship with God, the Holy Spirit, is that he produces his fruit—the fruit of the Spirit—in our lives. Remember, Paul says that the fruit of the Spirit is love, joy, peace, patience, kindness, goodness, faithfulness, gentleness, and self-control. The fruit is the evidence of Christian character and this character is what people saw when they observed the life of the incarnate Christ, who, we know, was filled and led by the Spirit. The point of all this is that when people—Christians or non-Christians—observe or examine our lives, they see the very character of Christ, as manifested by the fruit of the Spirit."

"And how does this relate to ministry?" Bob asked. "What does God want me to do?"

My Ministry

"The answer," Steve said, "is to serve him in ministry. He makes this very clear in Matthew 20:17–28." He flipped the worn pages of his Bible to Matthew. "You know the story. The mother of two of Jesus' disciples quietly approached him with her sons and asked that Jesus grant each of them positions of honor in his kingdom. Then in verse 24 it says that when the other disciples heard what they had done, they were incensed. At this point, the Savior intervened and called them together as a group and taught them the following." Steve read verses 25–27: "'You know that the rulers of the Gentiles lord it over them, and their high officials exercise authority over them. Not so with you. Instead, whoever wants to become great among you must be your servant, and whoever wants to be first must be your slave—just as the Son of Man did not come to be served, but to serve, and to give his life as a ransom for many.'"

Steve looked at Bob. "This is the answer to your question. Our lives and ministries must be summed up in one word—*service.* That's where our gifts and talents come into the picture. God has invested us with abilities so that we might serve him and his people."

Bob nodded and wrote something on his notepad.

The Tools of Character and Ministry

"Second," Steve continued, "we need to probe the components or tools of character and ministry."

The Tools of Character

"The components of our character are our heart, soul, and spirit. All three of these terms are used in certain contexts to refer to the immaterial part of our being. *Heart* is used to refer to not only the organ in our chest but also to our will in 2 Corinthians 9:7 and as a synonym for the mind in Matthew 15:19 and Psalm 119:11. The concepts of soul and spirit are complex and often difficult to distinguish. The difference between the two seems to be one of function, although even the functions appear to overlap at times. The soul is to love God and stand against sinful desires that war against it. In Hebrews 13:17 the writer enjoins us to submit to our leaders and obey their authority because they keep watch over us. The word translated 'you' in this verse is literally 'soul.' They keep watch over our souls. And in Romans 8:16 the Holy Spirit appears to work through our human spirit, but Paul warns, in 2 Corinthians 7:1, that our spirit can be contaminated. Let's read Hebrews 4:12," Steve said, turning the pages of his Bible. "This passage brings the three concepts of heart, soul, and spirit together in one verse and explains how Scripture affects them: 'For the word of God is living and active. Sharper than any double-edged sword, it penetrates even to dividing soul and spirit, joints and marrow; it judges the thoughts and attitudes of the heart.' All three tools seem to impinge in some way on the Christian's character. Therefore it is imperative that we be involved in heart and soul work as well as ministry work."

"In other words, that's how we develop godly character," Bob said.

"Correct," Steve agreed.

The Tools of Ministry

"Now for the tools of the ministry," Steve continued.

"Aren't they the gifts, talents, and abilities we talked about earlier?" Bob interrupted.

"That's right. Can you give some scriptural support?" Steve asked.

Bob nodded. "It's easy. For example, in the area of spiritual gifts, the passages work together: Romans 12 along with 1 Corinthians 12 and Ephesians 4 with 1 Peter 4. So this means our heart and soul work precedes the development of our gifts, talents, and skills!"

"That's correct," Steve said. "I suspect that in reality, they both work together, but our heart and soul work must be emphasized over the development of our abilities because we are so prone to reversing the order. Our natural tendency is to become so involved in the exercise of our gifts, talents, and skills in ministry that we neglect or forget about the need to cultivate our heart and soul."

God's Role in Developing Character and Ministry

"Let's take a little break," Steve said as he stood and stretched. He took a bag of hard candy from his desk drawer and offered some to Bob. When they sat back down, Steve began talking about God's role in developing character and ministry. "We need to understand," he said, "that character concerns what God does *in us* as objects of his grace, while ministry concerns what he does *through us* as vehicles of his grace."

God's Role in Our Character

"What does God do in us as grace recipients?" Steve continued. "Scripture elaborates four things. First, God both initiates and carries out good works in our lives. That's what Philippians 1:6 says." Steve quoted the verse, "'He who began a good work in you will carry it on to completion until the day of Christ Jesus.' Look at verse 5—the context of this passage—it appears that one good work is 'our partnership in the gospel.' God also works in us so that we both desire and then accomplish his good purpose." Steve turned the page of his Bible. "In Philippians 2:13 Paul writes: 'For it is God who works in you to will and to act according to his good purpose.' And he uses the Holy Spirit to form Christ in us, as we saw in Galatians 4:19. Finally, he renews us inwardly and that serves to strengthen us during times of affliction. You know the 2 Corinthians 4:16–17 passage: 'Therefore we do not lose heart. Though outwardly we are wasting away, yet inwardly we are being renewed day by day. For our light and momentary troubles are achieving for us an eternal glory that far outweighs them all.'"

Bob was still writing but nodded as Steve read the verses.

God's Role in Our Ministry

As Steve pointed to the next item in his chart, he asked, "What does God do through us as grace vehicles?" Then he answered his own question. "Scripture mentions several things. First, as Christ's ambassadors, God appeals to the hearts of lost people through us, inviting them to be reconciled to him. We see this in 2 Corinthians 5:19–20: 'And he has committed to us the message of reconciliation. We are therefore Christ's ambassadors, as though God were making his appeal through us.'" Steve emphasized *through us* and continued reading. "'We implore you on Christ's behalf: Be reconciled to God.' The second thing God does is to exalt Christ through our bodies both in life and death. Philippians 1:20 says, 'I eagerly expect and hope that I will in no way be ashamed, but will have sufficient courage so that now as always Christ will be exalted in my body, whether by life or by death.'"

"Hmm. That's interesting," Bob said, rereading the verse.

Our Role in Developing Character and Ministry

Then Steve pointed to the third row of the chart. "Not only do we need to understand God's role in our character and ministry development, but we must understand our role as well. Our responsibility to God in the area of character is *to be with him,* whereas in the area of ministry we are *to do for him.*"

Being with God

"What exactly do you mean when you say 'to be with him'?" Bob asked.

"I believe," Steve responded, "that the answer to your question is found in Mark 3:13–14 when Jesus appointed the twelve apostles. Mark writes, 'Jesus went up on a mountainside and called to him those he wanted, and they came to him. He appointed twelve— designating them apostles—that they might be with him and that he might send them out to preach.' Note that one purpose for his appointing the twelve was so they 'might be with him.' It's important to note that the Savior was in the habit of periodically withdrawing from the crowds either by himself for prayer or with his disciples for personal time with them. For example, Mark tells us in chapter 1, verse 35, that on one occasion, 'Very early in the morning, while it was still dark, Jesus got up, left the house and went off to a solitary place, where he prayed.' He repeated this later according to Mark 6:46. And in Mark 3:7 it says that at another time 'Jesus withdrew with his disciples to the lake.' But this time a large Galilean crowd followed. We see much the same practice in Mark 6:31–32. So it should not surprise us to find Jesus situated on a mountainside with his future disciples—apparently away from the crowd—in Mark 3:13."

Steve flipped back to Mark 3. "This event recorded in verses 13 and 14 is a key event that marked the beginning of Jesus' personal time with, and the training and sending out of, the Twelve."

"What do you think took place when the disciples were alone with him?" Bob asked.

"The context of Mark's Gospel gives us some information. In Mark 4:13–20 and 34, he explained to them the meaning of the parables. He also used this time alone with them to strengthen their faith, such as when he stilled the storm in Mark 4:35–41."

"So," Bob laid his notepad and pen on the table, "when they were alone, Jesus was helping them gain insight into who he is."

"Exactly," Steve nodded. "When I speak of being with Jesus," Steve continued, "I'm talking about the urgent need for leaders to spend some quality quiet time alone with the Savior."

"Doing the same things with him as his disciples did?" Bob asked.

"Yes, by studying his Word and simply reading and absorbing the teachings of the Savior, especially as they are recorded in the Gospels. It involves letting the Savior speak personally to us through his Word by pausing and asking ourselves such questions as, What is he teaching and telling me about himself, myself, and life in general?

"Being with him also involves spending significant quality time with others," Steve added.

"What do you mean?" asked Bob.

"Evaluation is critical to our spiritual growth and maturity. Most often this takes the form of self-evaluation—we evaluate ourselves in isolation. That's often skewed subjectively—we're either too hard or too easy on ourselves."

"It's also safe!" Bob interjected.

"True," Steve agreed, "but there are some issues that can be addressed only in relationship. That's why we need to solicit insight from others—spouse, team-mates, close friends—if we're to get an objective read on our spiritual development. Other people see things that we often don't see but need to deal with for effective growth."

"How would you go about getting that kind of information?" asked Bob.

"I can think of several ways. Being vulnerable with your spouse, letting her give you honest feedback is one way. Doing the same with friends, perhaps meeting weekly in a safe group with close friends is another. A third way is risking vulnerability with your staff by allowing them to evaluate you."

"My problem," Bob concluded, "is that I allow my ministry activity to push aside my time alone with the Savior or with other people. I'm so anxious to do for him that far too often I don't have time to just be with him and his people."

Steve smiled. "I know what you mean. It's a problem that leaders must constantly be concerned with, because God does want us to *do*. Let's look at that."

Doing for God

"Not only did the disciples in Mark 3:14–15 spend time with the Savior," Steve went on, "but they ministered for him. This involved preaching, healing, casting out demons, and other ministries. This is our model. Not only do we spend time with him, but we minister, not for ourselves or in our own interests but for him. In 2 Corinthians 5:14–15, Paul appeals to Christ's love for us as demonstrated by the cross. This appeal involves living our lives only for him, 'And he died for all, that those who live should no longer live *for themselves* but *for him* who died for them and was raised again.' His death is our motive for service. According to Philippians 1:29, this also includes suffering for him while contending for the faith: 'For it has been granted to you on behalf of Christ not only to believe on him, but also to suffer for him.'"

"To be honest with you, Steve, my motives in my ministry for him are more often mixed than pure," Bob confessed. "Sometimes I think that I'm ministering for my own ends as well as, or instead of, his."

The half-smile on Steve's face said that he could identify with what Bob was saying. "I'm convinced that what is true of you is true of all of us in ministry. I believe that it was also true of those who served Christ back in the first-century church. Otherwise Paul wouldn't have had to say what he said. To me, this kind of awareness and confession are the first steps to personal integrity and authentic ministry for him."

The Relationship between Character and Ministry

"Now you can probably tell me how character and ministry should relate," Steve said as he pointed to the fifth row of the chart.

"Well," Bob said, "it seems obvious that an emphasis on character must precede doing ministry. Character comes first and ministry is second."

"You're right on," Steve nodded while turning to Acts 6 in his Bible. "We see this in the Scriptures. For example, remember in the early church the problem that surfaced between the Grecian and Hebraic Jews? The Grecian widows were being overlooked in the daily distribution of food. Note how the apostles chose to solve the problem. Rather than take the responsibility on themselves, as we might have a tendency to do, the apostles delegated it to seven men— but not just any seven. Before they commenced their ministry, the apostles clarified that the men had to meet certain character qualifications: They were to be full of the spirit, faith, and wisdom. These qualifications are similar to those given for elders and deacons in 1 Timothy 3:1–13 and Titus 1:6–9 that were used as a basis for selecting the elders (who I believe were the first-century pastors of the church) and the deacons who probably assisted them. Even in Mark 3:13–14 Mark indicates that the Savior appointed the Twelve, first, that they might be with him and, second, that they serve him. The order is most important. The principle is that character always precedes ministry."

"So that's why God chooses to do his work *in us* before he does his work *through us* in the lives of our people," Bob offered.

"Yes, and being an object of God's grace comes prior to being a vehicle of his grace," Steve added.

"And," Bob grinned as he looked through his notes, "being with him comes before doing for him!"

"That's certainly the point in Mark 3:13–14, isn't it?" Steve agreed.

The Temptation
of Character and Ministry

"Now we come to the temptation to neglect character and focus on ministry," Steve said as he glanced at his watch. "Yikes, where has the time gone? We'll have to cover this one quickly. Our gifts, talents, and skills, along with our abilities to do, present a temptation. We are tempted to assume that the development of character will take care of itself and that we must concentrate on developing our ministry. We see this both in the formal training of ministers today as well as in our own private preparation. Far too many seminaries and seminars that attempt to train people for ministry presume that somewhere along the way we have worked on the development of our character. So seminaries and seminar leaders tend to ignore this vital area, to the detriment of their students. Often seminaries focus on training students in the skills and capacities needed by leaders for ministry and emphasize preaching and exegesis. Seminars that are organized to teach leadership usually adhere to that strict agenda and avoid the issue of character development. Even in our private, personal preparation the temptation is to allow our heart and soul to shrivel while our gifts, talents, and skills grow."

Steve looked at his watch again and closed his Bible. "Well, I shouldn't hold you any longer," he said.

"Thank you, Steve. This was really good." Bob extended his hand to Steve. "I plan this week to monitor my character development time and my ministry accomplishment time. I already know that they're out of sync. My goal is to make some needed corrections before we meet next week to discuss the pastor and his leadership. Perhaps you could hold me accountable for my character development."

"And you, me," Steve suggested. They agreed, prayed together, and left each other to tackle the busy day that lay ahead for both of them.

Steve had given Bob a lot to think about. Bob could not avoid the realization that he had been focusing almost exclusively on *doing* ministry. He was so determined to do it right at Grace and he assumed that success would come only if he wore himself out on the many responsibilities he had taken on as senior pastor. He had begun to assure himself that the time he spent studying for his sermons, counseling with members on spiritual matters, and teaching Bible studies were ways through which God would develop his spirit. He hadn't noticed until now that his time of personal devotion had dwindled out of his daily schedule.

Bob left the session with Steve determined to make the needed changes. The first changes would have to be revising his daily schedule and rethinking his priorities. He decided to write into his daily planner his devotional time when he would be alone with God. This would be inviolable. He also planned to spend more time with others who could hold him accountable spiritually. The vitality of his heart and soul depended on it.

> For the fruit of the Spirit, see Galatians 5:22–23. For a discussion of the concepts of soul and spirit, see Charles C. Ryrie, *Balancing the Christian Life* (Chicago: Moody, 1969), 43. Also see Matthew 22:37 and 1 Peter 2:11, which talk about the soul.

Pastors and Their Leadership

Understanding What You Do

Bob and Steve pulled into the parking lot of Steve's church at the same time and walked into Steve's office together for their third session. It was early and they were the only people in the building. Steve started a pot of coffee and they sat in their usual chairs, facing each other.

Steve had noticed Bob's somber mood and asked him about it. "What's up, Bob? You don't seem to be your usual cheerful self!"

"Oh, I'm okay, Steve." Bob sighed. "It's just that I'm a little discouraged. I went away from our last session determined to make some changes in my personal devotional life." Bob shifted uneasily in his chair. "I guess I just haven't been as successful as I wanted to be and now we're going to talk about leadership." He glanced at Steve and then looked away. "I'm not sure I'm ready for this topic."

Steve smiled and nodded. "I know how you feel."

"You do?" Bob couldn't hide his surprise.

"Sure. I often feel inadequate, but I praise God for it because it reminds me of how completely I must rely on him if I am going to be a good leader of our people. I like to think about David and how he had to be corrected by God but turned out to be a great leader. Israel's leaders were like pastors. They were to shepherd the people just as we are. That's what it says in passages like Psalm 78:72; 2 Samuel 5:2; and Ezekiel 34:4–5." Steve paused and looked at Bob, trying to read his thoughts. "So let's move ahead with the topic of leadership. I think you'll see that the topics we discuss in each of our sessions together are, and should be, continuing concerns of every pastor. We don't master one area and then move on to the next, but we work on them all concurrently."

As Bob listened to Steve, he began to relax. He nodded in agreement as Steve suggested they pursue the topic of leadership.

"While it's never been easy to lead a church in any generation," Steve began, "during the 1980s and 1990s pastoral ministry became a leadership intensive enterprise. And there's no evidence that things will be any different in the twenty-first century. I think that this is due to a number of things. One is that we, as pastor-leaders, are facing sweeping, chaotic change, perhaps as never before in history. The western world is transitioning from a modern to a postmodern worldview and this has resulted in phenomenal changes in most every area of life. There is also a growing cynicism toward anyone involved in leadership—whether in politics, the marketplace, or the church. We touched on that last time. People tend not to trust us because other leaders have betrayed their trust. The fact that the mainline denominations and many evangelical churches are plateaued or in decline is another reason for the need for strong leadership in pastoral ministry. Church decline has been evident in western Europe and North America over the latter part of the twentieth century. In some places, churches sit empty. I contend that if the typical, born-before-the-1960s, traditional church checked into the hospital, they would put it on life support!" Steve joked.

Bob grinned as Steve went on, "A major problem that pastors—especially younger pastors who have seminary training—face in their ministry is the shifting pastoral paradigm."

Bob frowned. "What do you mean by that?"

"The typical pastoral model of ministry that is especially evident in small churches—and the majority of churches are small—is the one in which the pastor preaches and does most of the pastoral care. During seminary I pastored a small, older, somewhat rural-minded church that had been run over by urban expansion. They wanted someone to preach on Sunday morning and evening and to care for the members during the week. Caring meant an occasional wedding, many funerals, and much visitation, which involved visiting people in the hospital—they were horribly offended if I didn't—and visiting them in their homes—this always involved sampling Grandma's favorite dessert with lemonade or iced tea.

"However," Steve continued, "I noted that the professors in the seminary operated on a different pastoral model."

"Yeah, I think I know what you mean," Bob grimaced.

"Most of the courses focused on the one hour on Sunday morning. The practical departments viewed it as a preaching time, and the academic departments viewed it as a teaching time. The latter saw the pastor as a scholar who primarily functioned as a teacher in the pulpit. My problem with the scholar-pastor model is that it is theoretical. Few, if any, of the professors have ever pastored a church. The training in the exegetical skills, Bible knowledge, theology, and church history are, of course, a must. The problem is that most seminary students receive little training in leadership, except for an occasional seminar that happens to come to the area."

Bob was nodding enthusiastically. "Yes! That was my experience in seminary as well, except I didn't have time for the seminars!"

Steve laughed. "Me either! Now the emergence and growth of the megachurch movement have greatly encouraged the development of a new leadership model, that of leader-communicator. It is uncertain what this model will eventually look like. The pastors are strong, gifted leaders who are also skilled communicators. Some are also brilliant strategists, and many—having given up on the more traditional style church—are church planters. Following along in their footsteps are a number of younger, talented church planters who have embraced this model."

"So what is the correct leadership model?" Bob asked.

"I'm convinced that the Scriptures allow much freedom in this area, even though the tendency among some people has been to criticize severely the newer models, arguing that they aren't biblical. There is freedom but certain biblical imperatives provide what I refer to as timeless leadership functions. In the rest of today's session, I want to surface these functions by asking and answering three questions: Who were the leaders in the early church? What does it mean for pastors to be leaders? and How should leaders function as pastors?"

The Leaders in the Early Church

Steve reached behind him and took his Bible off his desk. He found the passage as he talked. "Let's try to answer the first question: Who were the leaders in the early church?"

Elders and Bishops

"The New Testament used two primary terms for the church's leaders—*elders* and *bishops* (or *overseers*). It would appear that both terms refer to the same leadership office. In Acts 20:17 Paul first addresses the leaders of the church at Ephesus as elders and then calls them overseers in verse 28. He does the same in Titus 1:5 and 7. It seems that the term *elder* was the name for the position and possibly depicts the dignity of the individual who filled it, while 'overseer' is referring to the leadership function of the office. Consequently today's pastors are probably the equivalent of the early church's elder-bishops." Bob looked perplexed but Steve hurried on.

Elders and Bishops as Pastors

"The evidence of the New Testament in general and Acts in particular points to a plurality of elders in each church. Here's a list of verses that support this." Steve handed Bob a card on which he had typed several Scripture references.

The Evidence for a Plurality of Elders

Acts 14:23	Acts 20:17	Acts 15:2
Philippians 1:1	Titus 1:5	James 5:14
1 Peter 5:2		

As Bob studied the list, Steve said, "It would be a mistake, however, to argue that, based on these verses, every church must have several elders. Some people assume that the churches in the first century were small like most churches today; therefore, elders would have included laymen who would be equivalent to today's church leadership board. But this wasn't necessarily the case. The church of the first century existed at two levels: city churches and house churches. Many of the churches in Acts were large city churches. For example, Acts 2:41 says that the Jerusalem church began with three thousand people and in Acts 4:4 it says that the number of men grew to around five thousand. The Jerusalem church probably met together as a city church at the temple courts in a large place reportedly called Solomon's Colonnade. Paul wrote some of his letters to these city churches.

"Due to persecution and for ministry purposes, each city church included several or many house churches. Though they met as separate fellowships, they were not viewed as different churches. They were all part of the larger city church. Consequently each house church may have been the size of today's typical small church and most likely had only one elder if any. While some probably were laypeople, the evidence is that the desire was for elders to lead the church and to be paid."

Steve jumped up and rummaged through a pile of papers on his desk. Finally he found what he was looking for and, sitting back down, handed it to Bob.

Jerusalem Church

Acts 1:15	a group numbering about a hundred and twenty
Acts 2:41	about three thousand were added to their number
Acts 2:47	added to their number daily
Acts 4:4	the number of men grew to about five thousand
Acts 5:14	more and more men and women . . . were added
Acts 6:1	the number of disciples was increasing
Acts 6:7	increase rapidly

Churches in Judea, Galilee, Samaria

Acts 9:31	grew in number
Acts 9:35	all those who lived at Lydda and Sharon . . . turned to the Lord
Acts 9:42	all over Joppa, and many people believed in the Lord.

Church at Antioch

Acts 11:21	a great number
Acts 11:24	a great number of people
Acts 11:26	great numbers

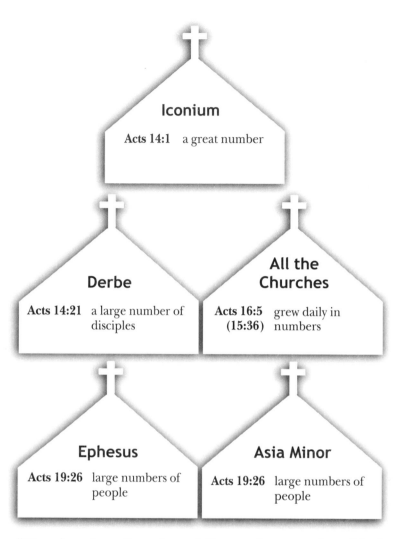

Iconium

Acts 14:1   a great number

Derbe

Acts 14:21   a large number of
disciples

All the Churches

Acts 16:5   grew daily in
(15:36)   numbers

Ephesus

Acts 19:26   large numbers of
people

Asia Minor

Acts 19:26   large numbers of
people

"Here's a chart I made a while ago for a seminar I led. I think it drives home my point."

"Wow, this is great," Bob exclaimed. "I've never heard this before, though it really seems to make sense. I'll want to study these passages and think over what you've said. I confess that I sure feel much better about being the only elder in my church. Some pastor friends had just about convinced me that being the only elder was unbiblical."

"My response," Steve interrupted, "is that they are free to do it their way, and you're free to do it your way. The Scriptures don't mandate the number of elders for any particular church."

Pastors as Leaders

Steve was ready to move on, so Bob slipped the chart into a folder he had started with his notes from the week before.

"The second question is, What does it mean for pastors to be leaders? A good definition of a leader is a godly servant who knows where he or she is going and has followers. Let's look at the various components of that definition."

"Wait a minute," Bob interrupted. "I want to get this definition written down."

A leader is a godly servant who knows where he or she is going and has followers.

Leaders Are Godly Servants

Steve waited until Bob finished writing. Then he continued, "The term *godly servant* is a reference to a leader's character. As we said last time, godly character is an essential requirement for a pastor who would be the leader of his church. Paul assumes this in 1 Timothy 3:1–7 and Titus 1:6–9 where he provides the qualifications for elders. The list of qualifications in both passages begins with a single, general qualification. In 1 Timothy 3:2 that general qualification is described as 'above reproach.' In Titus 1:6 it's 'blameless.' The broad qualifications are followed by specifics that seem to flesh out and explain the more general terms. In both passages Paul is looking for leaders of integrity.

"Some might judge these qualifications to be rather strict; however, they're the same characteristics as those of admired leaders in the marketplace, some or many of whom may not be Christians. I read that a joint survey conducted by Korn/Ferry International, a highly respected research firm, and the Columbia University School of Business reported that respondents look for their ideal chief executives to be literally 'above reproach.'"

"They actually used the same words as are used in Scripture?" Bob asked.

"Yes, isn't that interesting? The marketplace has discovered the value of servant-leadership as well as the church. Several writers who address leadership in the corporate world have begun to refer to them as servants first. So the attitude of leaders must be that of godly servants. They are to be servant-leaders according to Matthew 20:25–28."

"Our model, then, is Jesus," Bob said.

"That's right," Steve nodded. "Servant-leaders are givers more than takers. However, some pastors mistakenly assume that as servant-leaders they are to do all the work of the ministry. Theirs is an active-passive relationship with the congregation. They are in the church to serve people, and the people are there to be served. Some congregants assume this as well. But servant-leaders aren't in the church to do others' ministries for them. Their job is to work hard to provide others with the resources and working conditions they need to accomplish their ministry goals. They make others feel more important than themselves. They have others' best interests at heart.

"The classic passage defining servant-leadership is Philippians 2:3–8: 'Do nothing out of selfish ambition or vain conceit, but in humility consider others better than yourselves. Each of you should look not only to your own interests, but also to the interests of others.'" Then to make his point, Steve continued, "Paul provides the example of Christ: 'Your attitude should be the same as that of Christ Jesus: Who being in very nature God, did not consider equality with God something to be grasped, but made himself nothing, taking the very nature of a servant, being made in human likeness. And being found in appearance as a man, he humbled himself and became obedient to death—even death on a cross!' Again, Christ is our model."

Leaders Know Where They're Going

Steve glanced at Bob to see if he was ready to move on. He was. "A second component of the definition of a leader," Steve said, "is that he or she is a godly servant who knows where he or she is going. The leader knows the direction of his or her life as well as where he or she is leading the church. There is both a personal and corporate direction. The personal direction is the leader's own mission and vision in life. The corporate direction is the mission and vision of the leader for the church." Steve paused, gathering his thoughts. "As you know, the church's mission is the Great Commission, found in Matthew 28:19–20. The church doesn't need to debate where it's going, Christ predetermined its direction more than two thousand years ago: Its purpose is to 'make disciples.' The church's vision comprises the leader's vision for the fulfillment of the church's purpose in the ministry community. We'll look at this again when we talk about the leader and the church."

"Good," Bob said. "I'm not sure I understand the difference between the mission and the vision of the church."

Leaders Have Followers

"For now, though," Steve continued, "let's finish looking at my definition. A godly servant-leader who knows where he or she is going will have followers. That's summed up in one word—*influence*. When leaders say, 'Follow me,' and they turn and look behind them, they should see people. You can say, 'I'm a leader,' but if no one is following you, then you're not a leader." Bob chuckled in agreement. "In Matthew 4:18–22 Jesus called Simon, Andrew, James, and John to follow him. When he turned and looked back, they were there and remained there for life."

"That's true," Bob said. "But that's Jesus. How do other leaders have influence?"

"Actually, I think the first two components of the definition of a leader explain why they have influence. First, true godliness has a magnetic effect on others. A person with godly character will attract followers. People are looking for leaders of integrity and when they find one, they're quick to climb on board for the voyage. Also, people who know where they're going will attract followers. So few people, even pastors, seem to know where they're going in life. Thus when someone shows a strong resolve to move in a particular direction, he or she will attract followers. People who combine these two components—strong character and clear direction—exert the strongest influence on people. When these leaders turn around and look, they always find people lined up to follow them."

"Of course at the same time, Christian leaders must point away from themselves to Christ, the one whom they themselves are following, so that people ultimately follow the Savior," Bob added.

Steve agreed. "As John the Baptist said in John 3:30, 'He must become greater; I must become less.'"

How Leaders Function as Pastors

Steve leaned back in his chair and stretched his arms over his head. "Ready to move on?" he asked.

Bob nodded, though he was still writing on his notepad.

Steve went on. "The third question, then, is, How should leaders function as pastors? Scripture teaches that all leaders as pastors are responsible for three functions. These are three timeless imperatives that characterize a pastor's ministry whether it's in the first or in the twenty-first century, whether it's a traditional or contemporary church. I use the term *imperative* because the Scripture passages are prescriptive commands and, therefore, offer better arguments for a function of a pastor than do descriptive passages that merely describe what leaders did. We'll look at some descriptive passages too."

Leaders Lead the Congregation

"The first timeless function of pastors is leading the congregation. Let's look at Acts 20:28. Paul delivers the elders of the church at Ephesus a timeless imperative. He commands them, 'Keep watch over yourselves and all the flock of which the Holy Spirit has made you overseers.' We talked earlier about the term *bishop*, that refers to the leadership function of elders and means 'to oversee.' Keeping watch over or overseeing the flock is a leadership function."

Steve again read from his Bible: "'Be shepherds of the church of God, which he bought with his own blood.' David and others in the Old Testament were shepherds of a nation or people. That meant they were to lead or rule them. Peter proves the point when he addresses the elders of the churches in Asia Minor and commands them in 1 Peter 5:2, 'Be shepherds of God's flock that is under your care, serving as overseers.' Then he adds qualifiers. Look at verse 3, 'not lording it over those entrusted to you.' He's talking about leadership.

"When the Scriptures present qualifications for a position, then that too is a strong argument for the perpetuation of a function such as leadership. One of the characteristics in 1 Timothy 3:4 that qualifies one to be an elder is leadership of one's family. The term that is used in verse 4 is translated 'manage' but it's one of several New Testament terms for what leaders do. Then, using the same term as he used in 1 Timothy 3:4, Paul asks in verse 5, 'If anyone does not know how to manage [lead] his own family, how can he take care of God's church?'"

Steve turned a page in his Bible. "Then in 1 Timothy 5:17, Paul, while teaching that the church is to pay its leaders, describes one of their functions." He read: "'The elders who direct the affairs of the church well.'"

"So directing the affairs of the church is a part of leadership?" Bob asked.

"Yes, but this is one of those descriptive passages concerning leadership and therefore doesn't argue for the perpetuity of a function as biblical imperatives do."

"That's right," Bob added. "You said they simply describe what took place."

"But in this case it's instructive because it describes how elders functioned in the first century."

Leaders Protect the Congregation

Steve moved on to the second timeless function. "The next timeless function is protecting the congregation."

"Really?" asked Bob. "I have to protect them too?"

Steve grinned and studied Bob's face. He didn't know if he was joking or not. "Look at Acts 20:29–31 where Paul warns the elders that they will face savage wolves—those who would 'distort the truth in order to draw away disciples.' Then he commands, 'So be on your guard! Remember that for three years I never stopped warning each of you night and day.' It's interesting how carefully Scripture warns Christians not to heed false teaching. Practically every Epistle warns of false teachers who would distort God's truth. And the elders as overseers were responsible to see that this didn't happen because they would and should have a better knowledge of truth than the average Christian in the church."

"Oh, I can see that," Bob said. "Elders definitely should protect the people from false teaching."

"Right. So protecting the flock is also an aspect of one of the qualifications for being an elder and leader. In Titus 1:9 Paul says that elders must hold firmly to the truth and one of the reasons is so that they can 'refute those who oppose it.'"

"Another good reason for really studying the Word," Bob added.

"Yes," Steve agreed. "We find an example of the elders involved in this very thing in Acts 15 where the church in Jerusalem met to clarify the gospel. Remember how the elders and the apostles met to determine whether a person had to become a cultural Jew to be saved?"

Bob nodded. "Yes, that was when a contingent was teaching that Gentiles must be circumcised to be saved."

"Yes. Peter, Paul, and Barnabas argued that this was not necessary for salvation. James quoted Scripture and they won the day."

Some Leaders Teach the Congregation

"The third timeless function is teaching the congregation. Outside of commands to Timothy to teach the Word in 1 Timothy 4:11 and 2 Timothy 4:2, Scripture doesn't command elders to teach the Scriptures unless it's implied in certain passages. For example, Paul may imply this in Acts 20:28 when he commands the elders of Ephesus to keep watch over the flock and to 'be shepherds to the church of God.' Regardless, in 1 Timothy 3:2 Paul indicates that one of the qualifications to become an elder was that they be 'able to teach.' The idea here is that they be 'skillful in teaching.'

"I believe the reason the Bible doesn't command all elders to teach the flock—only to be able to—is that not all elders functioned as teachers. First Timothy 5:17 indicates that while all elders were leaders, only some preached and taught. Bob, do you want to read that?"

Bob found the verse and read it, "'The elders who direct the affairs of the church well are worthy of double honor, especially those whose work is preaching and teaching.' Are you saying that leading the flock and protecting the flock are two timeless functions for all elders, but teaching the flock applies only to some of the elders?" Bob asked.

"Exactly." Steve nodded. "Most likely in the early church it was those elders with teaching gifts who did the teaching, although Scripture doesn't say that explicitly."

Leaders Function in Other Areas

"So the responsibilities of elders are leading, protecting, and teaching," Bob summarized.

"Yes, but Scripture indicates that elders did other things as well."

"I was afraid of that!" Bob grinned.

Steve smiled and continued. "For example, James, in 5:14, commands the Jewish Christians in Babylon and Mesopotamia to call the elders of the church to pray over them when they are sick. The implication is that the elders would comply. In 1 Thessalonians 5:12 the leaders were to admonish their people. If these were elders, then that was another responsibility. I'm sure that the elders served in other ways as well. Scripture repeatedly uses shepherd imagery when it talks about their responsibilities. The shepherd had a number of responsibilities, such as leading, protecting, watering, feeding, naming, and knowing the sheep. So it's possible elders may have been involved in other ministries. But those other ministries weren't imperative or required. However, leading, protecting, and teaching—for some—were the primary timeless functions.

"Well, Bob, that's it—a quick overview. We could spend a lot more time on this topic but we will need to move on."

"That's okay, Steve. This has been very helpful and I want to spend some time rereading these Scripture passages," Bob said, referring to the following chart he had made of the verses Steve had referenced.

Timeless Pastoral Functions

	Leading	Protecting	Teaching
Imperative	Acts 20:28 Hebrews 13:7,17	1 Peter 5:2	Acts 20:29–31
Character-istics of Leaders	1 Timothy 3:4–5	Titus 1:9	1 Timothy 3:2
Descriptive	1 Timothy 5:17 1 Thessalonians 5:12	Acts 15:2, 4, 6, 22, 23	1 Timothy 5:17

Bob again felt challenged by what Steve had taught him.

"I feel pretty good about my teaching abilities, but I know I have a lot to learn about being a leader," he confessed.

"You did say, though," Steve responded, "that you are a visionary."

Bob nodded.

"And you are a godly man and from what I've observed, you have a servant's attitude. So you've fulfilled two-thirds of the definition of a leader." He smiled at Bob, letting his words sink in. Then he asked, "Have you looked behind you lately?"

"What?" asked Bob, confused. He almost turned around in his seat and then he understood what Steve meant. "Oh, yeah," he said grinning. "Actually, you know, the people at Grace seem eager to follow me. They just seem to be waiting for me to tell them what to do!" Bob drained an imaginary drop of coffee from his empty cup, feeling embarrassed as he talked about himself.

"You've got all three parts, Bob! You're a leader!" Steve announced. "I hope our sessions together will help you feel more comfortable with the responsibilities of that role."

"I'm sure they will, Steve. I already feel that I'm beginning to know the direction I'm supposed to be heading."

"Good!" Steve clapped Bob on the shoulder as they both headed for the door.

Robert L. Saucy suggests that the term *elder* was the term used in the early church to designate the leadership position. See his book *The Church in God's Program* (Chicago: Moody, 1972), 142.

Concerning the city churches and house churches of the early church, see Rex Koivisto, *One Lord, One Faith* (Wheaton: Victor, 1993), 27–28.

For references to the Jerusalem church meeting at the temple courts, see Acts 2:46; 5:21, 42.

For references to the house churches of the early church, see Acts 12:12; Romans 16:3–5; 1 Corinthians 16:19; Colossians 4:15; and Philemon 1:2.

For a discussion of the survey conducted by Korn/Ferry International and Columbia University, see James M. Kouzes and Barry Z. Posner, *Credibility* (San Francisco: Jossey-Bass, 1993), 15.

Concerning David and others who were shepherds of Israel, see 2 Samuel 5:2; Psalm 78:72; and Ezekiel 34:1–10.

For information on what leaders are to do in the church, see 1 Timothy 5:17 and 1 Thessalonians 5:12.

Concerning the meaning of the phrase "able to teach" in 1 Timothy 3:2, I consulted Walter Bauer, *A Greek-English Lexicon of the New Testament and Other Early Christian Literature,* by William F. Arndt and F. Wilbur Gingrich (Chicago: University of Chicago Press, 1957), s.v. "didaktikos," 190.

Three

Pastors and Their Churches

Answering the Core Ministry Questions

"I usually come here about once a week," Steve said, as he and Bob slid into their seats in a relatively quiet corner of a fast-food restaurant. Steve had his usual cup of black coffee, and Bob had ordered a pancake breakfast. "As nice as my office is, I still find that I need an occasional change of scenery. I often come here toward the end of the week and sit, watch people, and pray."

"Hmm. I never thought about just observing people," Bob said, pouring syrup on his pancakes.

"It's amazing what you can learn," Steve said. "I think that pastors have to be careful about becoming isolated from people. Not the people in the church, but the people outside the church—whom some call the unchurched—most of whom don't know Christ. We need to understand them, their desires, and their needs. I pray for them and when I have the opportunity I ask them questions."

"Such as?"

"Such as, who are they, what are their hurts, what are their goals, and, most important, what would it take for my church to reach them?"

Bob responded, "Sounds to me like you have the gift of evangelism."

"No, but I'm convinced that most pastors, even if they don't have the gift of evangelism, should place evangelism high on their list of priorities for the church's ministry. I believe a church that doesn't reach lost people has missed to a great extent Christ's Great Commission mandate and God's heart for its ministry."

"If you're correct, and I suspect you are," Bob reflected with concern, "then I pastor such a church."

"Which brings me to our topic for this week," Steve said. "Let's focus this morning on pastors and their churches. I sense from what you've shared in passing that you're experiencing what I call the fog factor."

"What's that?" asked Bob.

"Well, you've said that you have tried to develop a mission and strategy, but you're not satisfied with them.

Something doesn't click, but you don't know what it is. It's not coming together. It's as if a fog has settled in over your thinking."

Bob nodded. "Yeah, exactly."

"I've looked over your mission and strategy and I feel good about what you've done, but I believe that some fundamental concepts are missing. My goal is to help you think through a few of the core concepts that all pastors must work through in ministry. The absence of these core concepts creates a sense of fogginess about what the church is doing. I too experienced the fog factor, so I know what you're feeling."

Steve continued, "This morning we'll ask and answer some fundamental questions that every church must ask about itself and its ministry for God. These are questions that most church leaders have asked consciously or unconsciously when first planting the church. However, over time the answers become lost in all the busyness of ministry. These questions deal with such vital ministry concepts as core values, mission, purpose, vision, and strategy. There are several questions concerning these concepts that should be asked. We will try to deal with three questions this morning."

The Values Question

Steve could tell by the look on Bob's face that he had touched on an apparent need that Bob had felt deep within for some time. Bob had finished his pancakes. He pushed the tray aside and took his notepad out of his folder. Steve continued, "The first question is the values question: Why do we do what we do?"

The Importance of Values

"Every ministry has certain durable core values that are ministry defining. They're important because they're fundamental to everything the organization does."

"What does that mean?" Bob asked, looking puzzled.

"Several things. Your values have everything to do with your church's distinctiveness, that is what distinguishes it from the church down the street. A church's distinctiveness attracts some people and not others. Also a ministry's core values determine the personal involvement of people. If their core values align with those of the church, then they are more likely to become involved and invest their life in the ministry. And core values communicate the church's bottom line or 'what's important around here.' They express what the church believes is God's heart for the ministry. These values become hidden motivators for people who share the values, and inspire them to active ministry. And core values provide a basis for the evaluation of a ministry. I was working with the pastor and board of a church in the area, and we did an exercise that helped them discover their church's actual values. They were appalled. Their actual values weren't what they should be and they realized they had much work ahead of them to develop the right values.

"Another aspect of values is their influence on the church's overall behavior. For example, they dictate every decision that is made and every dollar that is spent."

"Now that really gets my attention!" Bob exclaimed. "We make lots of decisions and do a good job of spending money, but I'm not so sure why we make those decisions or spend money as we do. You're saying that values are important. They are a major factor in why we do what we do."

"Precisely," Steve said.

"Here is what I've written down, Steve." And Bob read the following:

The Importance of Core Values

1. Values determine ministry distinctives.
2. Values dictate personal involvement.
3. Values communicate what's important.
4. Values inspire people to action.
5. Values aid ministry evaluation.
6. Values influence overall behavior.

"That's it," Steve said when Bob finished reading.

"Okay, now explain to me exactly what you mean by core values."

The Definition of Core Values

"Core values," Steve explained, "are the constant, passionate, biblical core beliefs that drive the ministry. As we take this definition apart, examine its parts, and put it back together, I think its meaning will become clearer."

"Say that again, Steve." As Steve repeated the definition, Bob wrote it down:

> Core values are the constant, passionate, biblical core beliefs that drive the ministry.

Constant

Steve began to explain the definition. "First, values are constant. While things around us are changing, your ministry's values shouldn't change appreciably. If they did change significantly, the result would be chaos in the church. Luke has recorded the Jerusalem church's core values in Acts 2:42–47." They both turned to the passage. Then Steve continued. "The Jerusalem church's core values are expository teaching, fellowship, prayer, biblical community, praise and worship, and evangelism. These were the church's bottom line, what it stood for. They served to help the church navigate the turbulent seas of transition that were swirling all around them during the first century. Had they suddenly decided to change one of them, such as evangelism, the result would have left followers confused, bewildered, and angry: 'One day you want us to reach lost people, and the next it's not important anymore. That's inconsistent!'"

Bob smiled and nodded. He understood.

Passionate

"Second, core values are passionate. *Passion* is a feeling word. It means that you feel strongly about these values. You and your church have numerous values—perhaps a hundred or more. But the questions to ask are, Which values stir our emotions? Which ones do we feel strongly about? The answers will identify your core values."

"I've identified one of yours already," Bob said.

"Yes? Which one?" Steve asked, frowning at Bob.

"Evangelism. I think you are passionate about getting to know people and their needs."

"You're right, Bob. That definitely is one of my passions! So you're beginning to understand what core values are?"

"Yes, I am. Just keep it simple." Bob chuckled.

Biblical

"Okay, this is pretty simple. Third, core values are biblical. That means that most likely they're sourced somewhere in the Bible."

"Like evangelism," Bob said. "Not only was it a value of the Jerusalem church, but it's found throughout the New Testament."

"Good example, Bob. I guess we can move on to the fourth part."

Beliefs

"Core values are core beliefs. If you were to list all the church's values, there would be many. Some, however, influence your people more than others. These are your core values. They're also your beliefs—your ministry's fundamental convictions or intrinsic precepts that define it—just as the Jerusalem church's values in Acts 2 tell what defined them."

Drive the Ministry

"Finally, core values drive the ministry. They sit in the driver's seat of the ministry vehicle. They quietly, often imperceptibly, move the ministry in a particular direction or, better, strongly influence that direction."

"Hmm, back to evangelism," Bob said. "The fact that evangelism is one of your core values and one of your church's must be a major reason why your church has seen a significant number of people come to faith over the last decade."

"I think that's right," Steve agreed. "Sounds to me as if you've captured the essence of what values are all about."

"Yes, I think so," Bob said, "but the obvious questions become, What are my church's values? How can I discover what we value?"

"We're going to talk about that," Steve said, "but we must cover one other item first."

The Kinds of Values

"There are different kinds of values, and I want to mention several. It's important to understand the differences. Here's a list I made." Steve handed Bob a sheet of paper on which he had typed the following:

The Kinds of Values

Conscious vs. Unconscious

Shared vs. Unshared

Personal vs. Organizational

Actual vs. Aspirational

Good vs. Bad

"First are conscious and unconscious values. Most churches hold many of their values at an unconscious level. They're not aware of them, nor can they articulate them. The job of a pastor is to move those values or beliefs to a conscious level so that your people, like the Jerusalem church, know what drives them. This involves values discovery, which we'll cover next. Then there are shared versus unshared values. Shared values are those that the church people hold in common, which lead to making a difference for Christ. Unshared values are those the people differ over and this leads to all kinds of problems."

"Yes, I know all about that," Bob said, without looking up from his writing.

"Common cause obviously starts with shared values," Steve added. "The third set of the list are personal versus organizational values. You and each person in your church have individual, personal values for the organization. When you put them together, they make up the church's organizational values."

"It would be important, then," interrupted Bob, "for my personal values for the church I pastor, or would consider pastoring, to agree with the church's values."

"That's correct," Steve nodded. "I call that values alignment. If the pastor's personal values for the organization differ significantly from the church's values, the pastor will be in for a hard time."

Steve pointed to actual versus aspirational values on the list. "The actual values are those beliefs that you and the church own and act on daily. The aspirational beliefs are those that you don't own or live by but would like to. Actual values represent what's true about you; aspirational values represent what could be true. And finally, good versus bad values. I think they're self-explanatory. For example, Ananias, in Acts 5:1–6, valued himself and his own interests above those of Christ and the believers who made up the Jerusalem church. That's a bad value."

The Discovery of Values

"Now we're ready for values discovery," said Steve.

"Good!" Bob said. "As you were talking, a few possibilities came to mind, but I need to know how to be sure they are my church's values."

"I can give you five ways that we used at my church to discover our values," Steve began. "The first is to write down what you think they are on a piece of paper. That's a 'cold turkey' or more difficult approach because you have to come up with them from 'out of nowhere.' The second is to take a core values audit. Here's one I've used that I think you'll find helpful." Steve handed Bob a document of several pages. "The third is to examine your budget," Steve continued. "Most churches' values drive their budgets.

"You could also collect and review other churches' credos or core values statements."

"How would that help in the discovery process?" Bob asked.

"Many find that when they scan the credos of others, certain values seem to leap off the page. I believe what's happening is that they're emotionally identifying with the values that are theirs. So it's another way to discover your own values. The fifth way is for you and your ministry team—staff, board, and other leaders—to discover them together. I met initially with my board and staff, and we discovered our values through a process called storyboarding. It involves asking for all in the group to express what they believe to be the church's values—that's called brainstorming. This results in forty to sixty values. Then as a group you must narrow them down to the church's eight to ten core values by asking each person to pick what they believe to be the primary beliefs. Did you get all that?" Steve asked.

"Yes," Bob said as he read aloud from his notes:

Core Values Discovery

1. Write down what you believe are your core beliefs.

2. *Take a core values audit.*
3. *Examine your budget.*
4. *Collect and review other ministries' credos.*
5. *You and the team discover your values together through storyboarding and brainstorming.*

"I assume, then, that you've done some of these and have developed a values credo for your church," Bob said.

"Yes, we have." Steve was looking in his briefcase. "Here's a copy for you."

"Great." Bob took the document and began to study it. "Grace needs to come up with something like this. I'm going to try the storyboarding method with my leadership team. I may need your help along the way."

"That's fine," Steve said. "Just ask."

"And will you have time to critique the finished product?" Bob asked.

"I'm sure I will, even if we just talk about it by phone. Look, while you're reading that, I'm going to get more coffee. Do you want some?"

"Sure," Bob said, not looking up from his reading.

When Steve came back with the two coffees, Bob was still engrossed in Northpoint's credo, but he soon slipped it into his folder.

The Mission Question

"Okay, let's move to the second fundamental question," Steve said. "I call it the *mission* question. It asks the church, What are we supposed to be doing?"

The Importance of the Mission

Bob flipped a page on his notepad and began writing.

Steve went on. "Mission is important for several reasons. First, it's directional. It provides the church with a compelling sense of direction so that everyone knows where the church is going. Second, a mission is functional. It answers the important question, What has God called us to do? Third, it presents the church's preferred future, so no one has to guess at its future. Within God's sovereignty, you can have a part in creating your ministry's future by determining its mission. Fourth, mission shapes the church's strategy. The mission answers the *what* question—What are we supposed to be doing? The strategy answers the *how* question—How will we accomplish the mission? A strategy makes no sense without a mission. Fifth, a mission facilitates evaluation. If you want to know how your church is doing, then evaluate whether or not it's accomplishing its mission."

Bob had written the following:

The Importance of a Mission

1. It dictates the ministry's direction.
2. It focuses the ministry's function.
3. It presents its preferred future.
4. It shapes its strategy.
5. It facilitates evaluation.

The Definition of the Mission

"All this makes good sense," Bob interrupted, "but what exactly do you mean by the term *mission?* We did some work on this in seminary. I'm wondering if you're using the same definition."

"I define a mission as a broad, brief, biblical statement of what the ministry is supposed to be doing," answered Steve.

"Okay, let me get that down." Bob wrote:

> *A mission is a broad, brief, biblical statement of what the ministry is supposed to be doing.*

"Could you break that down for me, Steve?"

"Sure. First, the mission is broad in the sense that it serves as an overarching, comprehensive statement. All that you do should fall within the mission statement. But the statement must be brief."

"How brief?" Bob wanted to know.

"Well, Peter Drucker says, and I agree, that it should be short enough to fit on a T-shirt. That's one sentence; otherwise, no one will remember it. And the mission is biblical in that the mission is sourced in the Scriptures. In just a moment, I'll show you your church's mission in the Bible. And the mission is a statement. You would be wise to articulate it—to write it out as your mission statement. Finally, it's what the ministry is supposed to be doing."

"And how do you know what that is?" Bob asked.

"It's in the Bible: Matthew 28:19–20."

"Oh, sure," Bob said. "The Great Commission—'Go into all the world and make disciples . . .'"

"You see," continued Steve, "some two thousand years ago, the Savior predetermined every church's mission. He wants every church to make disciples. So we have to ask ourselves, What is our church doing? and Is what we're doing what we're supposed to be doing?"

The Difference between a Church's Mission and Purpose

"The question I had at seminary, that no one really ever addressed, was the difference between a church's mission and its vision," said Bob.

"We should also include the difference between its mission and its purpose," Steve added. "Several years ago, I wrestled with this very question. I did some research and came up with some answers. I brought along some of the charts I developed from my own study." He handed Bob two charts. "Like the church's values and mission, the church's purpose and vision also ask broad, fundamental questions. The purpose asks, Why does the church exist? Why is it here? The biblical answer is to glorify God. We see that in such verses as Psalms 22:23 and 50:15; Isaiah 24:15; Romans 15:6; 1 Corinthians 6:20 and 10:31. The purpose question is different from the mission question. The purpose is broader in scope and focuses more on God. Look at that first chart and you'll see the differences."

Bob read the chart.

Distinctions between a Church's Purpose and Mission

	Purpose	Mission
Question	Why do we exist?	What are we supposed to be doing?
Goal	To glorify God	To make disciples
Scope	Broad	Narrow
Focus	God	Disciples

"That really clarifies it," he said.

The Distinctions between a Mission and a Vision

"Now, let's think about vision," Steve said. "The fundamental questions that the vision asks are, What kind of church would we like to be? What picture comes to mind when we think about or envision our church two years, five years, even ten years from now? Look at the other chart comparing mission and vision."

Distinctions between a Church's Mission and Vision

	Mission	Vision
Definition	Statement	Snapshot
Application	Planning tool	Communication tool
Length	Short	Long
Purpose	Informs	Inspires
Activity	Helps people know	Helps people see
Source	Head	Heart
Order	First	Second
Focus	Broad	Narrow

Steve pointed to the first row of the chart. "First, whereas the mission is a written statement, the vision is a mental picture or snapshot of the church's future that the congregation carries in their mental wallets and purses."

Bob grinned at the concept and Steve continued. "Second, the mission is a planning tool—to plan the ministry's future. The vision is a communication tool—to communicate that future. Third, the mission is short, short enough to fit on a T-shirt. A vision is longer and may range from a paragraph to twenty pages or more."

Steve continued to point to each item on the chart as he spoke. "Fourth, whereas the purpose of the mission is to inform the church where they're going, the vision serves to inspire them to move in that direction. Fifth, the mission helps people know what the church is supposed to be doing. The vision helps people see it. If people can't see it, it won't happen. Now let's see." Steve counted the items on the chart until he got to *source*. "Sixth, the mission comes from the head—it's more intellectual in origin. The vision originates from the heart—it touches our emotions. Seventh is the order. Often leaders develop the mission first, then as they dream about implementing it, the vision comes into focus. And eighth, the mission is a broad, overarching statement of the church's future. The vision is based on the mission but is more narrow and presents the details of that future, including the strategy, target group, and geography involved.

"Is that clear?" asked Steve.

"Very. Thanks! Say, do you happen to have a copy of Northpoint's vision statement I could look over?"

Steve rummaged in his briefcase and not finding the statement said, "How about if I mail it to you?"

"That would be fine," Bob said.

The Development of a Mission Statement

"I did bring Northpoint's mission statement." Steve pulled an attractive, well-designed folder from his briefcase. The folder contained information about Northpoint Community Church, including its core values and its mission statement. Steve pulled out one piece of paper and placed it on the table in front of Bob. On it was written one sentence:

The mission of Northpoint Community Church is to help people develop into fully functioning followers of Christ.

"Wow! That's concise and to the point," Bob said. "How did you come up with that?"

"The leadership and I began, as Christ commands, with the Great Commission—'Make disciples.' However, when I asked the people in my church for the definition of a disciple, I got all kinds of answers. Consequently I knew that we would have to clarify what we mean when we use the term around our church. So we personalized the Great Commission for our church and came up with this mission statement. Note that we call a disciple a 'fully functioning follower of Christ.' While it needs some clarification for outsiders, such as yourself, it communicates to our people what we're about because we refer to it all the time. Being followers of Christ needs little explanation. The words *fully functioning* do need some explanation. We asked ourselves an important question: What would a fully functioning follower of Christ—a disciple—look like? How would we know one if we saw one? Our answer was the three Cs: conversion, commitment, and contribution. Fully functioning followers have been converted to Christ, have committed themselves to grow in Christ, and are contributing to Christ (they serve the body with their spiritual gifts, share their finances, and seek the lost)."

"I like that," Bob said. "The fog is beginning to lift." Steve smiled at Bob's reference to his fog metaphor. "I developed a mission statement for my church that wasn't anything like this. But I'm beginning to pick up on not only the product—your mission statement—but the process that you worked through to produce it. But one question. If someone in your church isn't a functional or fully functional follower of Christ, does that mean that he or she is spiritually dysfunctional?"

Both men laughed, and then Steve answered, "We may laugh, and we don't say it that way around the congregation, but the answer is yes."

"All joking aside, why did you use the words 'to help people' as opposed to something like 'develop people into fully functioning followers of Christ'?" Bob asked.

"It's interesting that you ask, because originally we did use those exact words: 'to develop people into fully functioning followers.' However, the more I thought about it, I realized that those words place all the responsibility on the leadership's shoulders rather than where it belongs—on the congregation's. We're not there to develop people but to help or assist them to develop themselves into Christ's disciples."

"Yes. That's good," Bob said. "I hadn't thought about that. Developing a concise, well-worded mission statement is not as easy as it seems."

"You're right," Steve nodded. "It actually was a pretty long process for us to refine our statement to what you see there. The important thing is to find the words that precisely express what you want to say."

"Again, I'd like to ask for your help in reviewing what we come up with," Bob said.

Steve agreed.

The Strategy Question

Steve glanced at his watch, looked at Bob, and said, "I think we have enough time left to talk about the third fundamental question, the strategy question: *How* will we accomplish our church's mission? Actually, the church's purpose and vision ask fundamental ministry questions too. But since I gave them such brief treatment, I'm not including them this time. In my church's case the strategy question was, Exactly how do we help our people become fully functioning followers of Christ? The answer is a carefully developed strategy, tailored precisely for our church."

Bob looked intently at Steve as he thought about what Steve had just said. "So, actually, the strategy is as important as the mission. Without a strategy, a church probably won't accomplish its mission," he concluded.

The Importance of the Strategy

"That's right," Steve agreed. "The church's strategy is very important for several reasons. First, the strategy is the vehicle that accomplishes the church's mission and also the vision. Without a clear, high-impact strategy, the church will never realize its mission. It won't produce disciples. Second, the strategy facilitates understanding. It helps your people understand why they're doing what they're doing: attending a worship service, a small group, a Sunday school class, and other meetings. These all contribute in some way to making disciples. People need to understand that contribution. Third, a strategy provides a sense of momentum. Your strategy is a disciple-making process that has clear, discernible steps. Your people need to know the step they're at. They can know where they have been, where they are now, and where they need to be in the process. That's momentum. And fourth, the strategy maximizes the ministry's energy. Without a clear strategy, the congregation's energy, like light from a lightbulb, goes in many different directions. The strategy, and the mission as well, acts like a laser to focus all that energy in a specific direction."

Bob had written the following in his notes:

The Importance of a Strategy

1. It accomplishes the mission.
2. It facilitates understanding.
3. It provides a sense of momentum.
4. It maximizes ministry energy.

The Definition of the Strategy

"Do you have a definition of *strategy*?" Bob asked.

"As a matter of fact, I do." Steve grinned. "Ready?" Bob nodded. His pen was poised, ready to write.

"A strategy is the process that determines how your church will accomplish its mission."

Bob wrote it down.

> *A strategy is the process that determines how your church will accomplish its mission.*

"Three terms are important in my definition," Steve continued. "They are *mission, process,* and *how.*"

Bob circled the words in the definition as Steve said them.

Mission

"Every good strategy begins with a mission—the overall goal or what the ministry is supposed to be doing. The problem is that while every church will have a strategy—good or bad—it may have lost its mission over the years. So every church needs periodically to conduct a mission audit: to ask, What is our strategy supposed to accomplish?"

"You mean you can have a strategy without knowing what your mission is?" Bob asked.

"That's right. Unfortunately that's where many churches are—just going through the motions, doing what they've been doing for years and not knowing why." Steve shook his head.

Process

"Let's go on to *process*. Disciple making is a process. It's taking people from where they are—lost or saved—

and moving them to where God wants them to be—saved and mature. You may want to check Ephesians 4:10–16; Colossians 1:28–29; and 2:6–7. This process is like moving people from prebirth to maturity. It's the ministry means to accomplish the ministry ends."

"That's good," Bob said. "We need to think of disciple making as a process. So many of us expect Christians to be instantly mature. It just doesn't work that way. But I've always had trouble getting people to grow. How do you do it?"

Steve pointed to the circled word *how* on Bob's notepad. "That's the third term I want to discuss."

"Oh, yeah, of course!"

How

"The mission asks the *what* question; the strategy asks the *how* question: How do you move people from prebirth or new birth to maturity?"

"So you develop a strategy to help people grow?" Bob interrupted.

"Right. You want to develop a church-wide program that provides a means for everyone to become a disciple. I say this because in the past many pastors would pick out a few promising, committed people and pour their life into them. That's too limited. We need a process that helps all our people come to faith and then move to maturity."

The Development of the Strategy

"This is a bit overwhelming," Bob admitted. "I never thought about articulating a strategy. I just thought doing what we do—preaching, teaching, seminars—would help people grow."

"They do," Steve said. "But if they aren't part of a well thought-out strategy, they may be rather hit or miss in their effectiveness. But don't be discouraged. You'll see that developing a strategy actually makes disciple making easier because, remember, it provides momentum."

"Oh, yeah." Bob flipped back in his notes to look at what he had written about the importance of a strategy.

From Mission to Strategy

"The key is asking what a disciple looks like," Steve said. "Remember, my church's mission is to help people become fully functioning followers of Christ, and the characteristics of such a person are the three Cs: conversion, commitment, and contribution. Those three Cs not only are vital elements of our strategy, but they help us make the transition from our mission into our strategy. We've built our programs around them. For instance, our worship service. Our people have told us that their lost friends won't come to any of our community groups. They want anonymity. But they will come to a worship service. So we've designed that time for both our people and their lost friends. And we've designed our community groups to accomplish commitment and contribution."

Charting Your Strategy

Bob looked puzzled, so Steve reached over, took Bob's pad, and wrote *Strategy*. Under that he wrote *Conversion, Commitment,* and *Contribution*. "Under these are the programs that are designed to encourage each process. He continued to write. Then he turned the pad around to show Bob.

Strategy

Conversion	Commitment	Contribution
Worship Service	Community Groups	Community Groups
Special Events	Christian Education Ministries	Service Groups

"Of course, this chart doesn't show all our programs," Steve explained, "but we do have a master chart that does. This allows us always to keep the big picture in front of us. Every ministry has a 'shelf life,' so once a quarter we review the programs on the chart to see what is and isn't contributing to making disciples. We also use it for balance. We look to see if each C has an appropriate number of programs under it to accomplish it."

A Visual

"We have created a visual that helps our members remember our strategy," Steve said. He took the pad back from Bob and sketched the following three-legged stool.

A Fully Functioning Follower of Christ

"This stool serves as a visual to help us communicate our strategy to people," Steve explained. "The seat rep-resents the disciple. Leg 1 is conversion. The first stage in becoming a fully functioning follower. We tell our people that just as one leg isn't sufficient to support a stool, so conversion isn't enough to make one a fully functioning follower. We do the same with leg 2. The stool is more stable with two legs than one; however, it's not stable enough. Fully functioning followers have all three legs on the ground at the same time: They are converted, committed, and contributing."

Bob smiled. "There goes all the fog! I see how it all comes together. That's a great illustration—not your drawing but the concept!"

They both laughed and Steve gave the notepad a little push, sending it back to Bob's side of the table. "Okay, no more drawings," he said. "But the visual does work well. When I've taught this material to people of other cultures, they've understood the concept of a three-legged stool. The visual is cross-cultural. I encourage you to develop a visual that will help your people understand your strategy. If the stool will serve your people as an illustration, you're welcome to use it.

"We're out of time," Steve said. "Let's pray. Then I have to run."

After prayer they walked to their cars together. "I'm really excited," Bob said. "I've got to find some time this week to begin to take my church through this process. It will be interesting to see what we come up with."

"It sure will," Steve agreed. "I think you'll find the process and the result invaluable to the life of your church."

There are at least nine fundamental questions concerning a church's ministry. Only three were dealt with in this chapter. For the others, see Aubrey Malphurs, *Advanced Strategic Planning* (Grand Rapids: Baker, 1999).

For an in-depth treatment of the topic of core values, see Aubrey Malphurs, *Values-Driven Leadership* (Grand Rapids: Baker, 1997). Also see appendix A of *Values-Driven Leadership* for sample credos.

See appendix A of this book for a core values audit and appendix B for Northpoint's core values statement.

For an explanation of the storyboarding process, see chapter 1 in Malphurs, *Advanced Strategic Planning*.

For what Peter Drucker says about a short mission statement, see Randy Frazee with Lyle E. Schaller, *The Comeback Congregation* (Nashville: Abingdon, 1995), 6.

See appendix C of this book for Northpoint's vision statement.

The reference for the description of fully functioning followers of Christ is Acts 2:41–47.

Pastors and Their People

Relating to the Congregation, Staff, and Board

It had been a tough week for Pastor Bob. He had started talking with some of his board members about working on mission and vision statements and about the need for a mission strategy. His excitement was quickly dissipated by their lack of enthusiasm about his ideas. He tried not to get discouraged and decided he just needed to keep talking to them about it until they understood the value of the process. But then a difficult staff problem came out of nowhere, making Bob feel on the defensive and alone. He hoped that spending two hours with Pastor Steve would help lift his spirits and renew his hope that his ministry at Grace would be effective.

Bob was running late and when he rushed into Steve's office, he found Steve at his desk, reading the newspaper and drinking his first cup of coffee. "Mornin'," he said as Bob sank into his usual chair. "Want some?" He raised his mug toward Bob.

"Yes, maybe it will wake me up! I'll get it," Bob said, pushing himself out of the chair. He walked to the shelf that housed the coffeepot and poured himself a cup, adding powdered creamer and sugar. He stood there for several minutes, motionless except for his hand moving a spoon through his coffee.

"Ready?" Steve finally asked.

"Oh, sure." Bob quickly retook his seat.

"What's up, Bob? You seem preoccupied."

"Well, I guess I am." He paused, not sure how to begin. "I think I mentioned that administration isn't one of my strengths. Here's what happened. Several months ago I came up with some nonbudgeted money to hire a part-time administrator. She's a young mother in the congregation with gifts and talents in administration. Before she and her husband started their family, she worked as an administrative assistant for a small business in the area. I was told that she was quite good at it, though she is strong willed. When she and her husband had their first child, she made the decision to quit work and stay home to raise their new baby. However, like many couples, they had become used to two incomes and found themselves coming up a little short financially. So I offered her a part-time administrative position at the church and agreed to work her hours around her need to be with her child.

"I thought things were progressing well. This past week, however, I discovered that she's committed an end run on me."

"What do you mean by 'end run'?" asked Steve.

"Well, she and I clashed over one of my recent decisions—whether or not to fire our intern who is acting as a youth pastor. She's convinced that he's incompetent. The church hired him before I arrived, and he admittedly has struggled. He's young and inexperienced. I think that I can help him improve with a little direction and I want to give him some time to develop. I told her I had decided to keep him on a trial basis for several months. She said little in response, and I thought the issue was resolved.

"This past week I discovered at our monthly board meeting that she had taken my decision to a board member who brought it up at the board meeting. He presented her side, and I had to defend my decision. I believe that she was wrong in not coming to me first and in going over my head to the board member. I also believe that the board member was wrong by not coming to me before bringing it up at the board meeting. Regardless, the situation is a mess, and I have to try to figure out how to straighten matters out. This should not have happened."

"Welcome to the ministry," Steve quipped.

Bob's half-smile, deep sigh, and raised eyebrows revealed his ambivalence this morning about being a pastor. "Why weren't you there to warn me about these things before I decided to become a pastor?" he asked.

Steve smiled but said nothing for a moment. Then, "I find the timing of this incident to be extraordinary. Our topic today is the pastor's relationship to his people: the congregation, staff, and board."

"Well, I certainly need to listen today," Bob said. "I really don't know what to do. I hope what we discuss will give me some ideas."

"I find that much confusion exists in churches over how people should relate to one another," Steve said. "Most churches have a structure in place that is reflected in an organizational chart. The chart is part of the church's bylaws that someone has filed away in some church filing cabinet. It's supposed to help with these matters.

"It's interesting that many marketplace organizations have chucked their organizational chart, arguing that it's a corporate straitjacket that creates more problems than it solves. Their mantra is: 'The best organization is no organization.' I disagree. Every organization must have some kind of structure to function. Otherwise you would have chaos. How can you call it an organization if there's no organization? In such Scriptures as 1 Corinthians 14:33 and 40 and Colossians 2:5, Paul makes it very clear that the church is to operate in an orderly way. That calls for organization."

"That's a good point," Bob said. "I never thought of those verses applying to more than the worship service, but I can see how they relate."

"Yes," Steve continued, "organization is important in every part of the church. I think that the problem for most churches lies with the typical organizational chart that's one-dimensional and effective in only a limited number of situations. So today, I want to accomplish two things. I want to explain our church's three dimensions and show how each has its own corresponding structure. And I want to use those structures as the basis for charting the relationships between the pastor and the congregation, staff, and board. Are you ready to write?"

"Yes." Bob pulled out his notepad and pen. "You've touched a felt need this morning. I want to capture everything."

The Three Dimensions of the Church

"Every church is multidimensional," Steve began, "not one-dimensional. Therefore, a single organizational chart isn't sufficient because it reflects only one dimension of the church. We have structured my church around three primary dimensions: The church as cause, corporation, and community. Each has a different structure that, in turn, reflects different relationships among those who make up the congregation, staff, and board.

Let's explore those dimensions and their structures first. We'll examine the relationships later."

The Church as Cause

"First, the church as cause. The idea is that the church exists for a cause, something bigger than itself that goes beyond itself. This includes such concepts as the church's purpose—to glorify God; its mission—the Great Commission; and the building of Christ's church."

Steve paused and then said, "I felt sorry for you and all your note taking, so I typed up some charts that summarize all the information I'm going to give you today." Steve handed Bob a chart titled The Church as Cause. "I included a lot of Scripture references that we won't have time to look up."

	The Church as Cause
Metaphor	God's army fighting the good fight Romans 7:23; Ephesians 6:10–18; Philippians 2:25; 1 Timothy 1:18; 6:12; 2 Timothy 2:3–4
Emphasis	Leadership Romans 12:8
Focus	Outward
Role of Christ	Commanding Officer 2 Timothy 2:3–4
Role of the pastor	Leader and fellow soldier 1 Timothy 1:18
Role of the people	Soldiers 2 Timothy 2:4
Primary emotion	Excitement
Condition of the church in its absence	Directionless

Bob took the chart, nodding his thanks, and studied it as Steve continued talking. "The metaphor for the church as cause is God's army fighting the good fight of faith and enduring hardship against the flesh and the powers of Satan so as to please its Commanding Officer. The church must have strong, gifted pastoral leadership that passionately communicates the cause and enlists followers—fellow soldiers—who feel challenged and are attracted to the cause. The leadership leads in the good fight for the faith and participates in the same.

"The focus of the church that has a cause is outward. Wars are to be fought, enemies to be vanquished, and captives to be freed. Christ would have us win souls, free those whom Satan has taken captive, and stand our ground against the assaults of the evil one. This outward focus is critical because so many churches over time turn inward and lose any sense of a cause greater than maintaining the ministry and keeping the doors open."

"Yes. I think that's where Grace is right now," Bob said.

Steve pointed to the fourth row on the chart. "Various roles surface within this military metaphor. The church's people serve as soldiers under their leaders. And they all serve to please God, who is their Commanding Officer. The senior or only pastor is a fellow soldier who at the direction of the Commanding Officer leads his troops into battle.

"The primary emotion that surfaces as the soldiers prepare to go into battle, defend their ground, or charge the hill for Christ is excitement. The church needs a sense of excitement, a sense that God is working in their midst, that they are making a difference in this world for Christ. It's exciting when soldiers see themselves growing and becoming more Christlike in the midst of the struggle. This makes the battle worth the effort and encourages the soldiers not to lose heart.

"When there is no cause, the church has no direction. The soldiers are fighting hard but don't know why. They ask, 'What's this war all about anyway?' The leadership responds, 'We don't know either but we've been fighting as long as we can remember.' Over time, their efforts diminish and may eventually cease altogether.

"We decided to represent the cause dimension of our church like this." Steve drew a diagram below the chart.

As Steve drew, he explained, "Christ is the Commanding Officer, and the pastor functions as his captain and the primary leader of the church. The pastor takes his orders from his Commanding Officer: 'Go, make disciples!' Under the pastor are the board, staff, and congregation. They look to the pastor as primary

Cause

Christ

Pastor

Board Staff

Congregation

leader to cast the vision, explain the cause, and challenge and influence them to join in the battle for the Savior."

"That's really an exciting and challenging picture of the church," Bob said.

The Church as Corporation

Steve handed Bob another chart. "We're ready to move on to the second dimension, which is corporation. The Scriptures describe the church as an organization.

The metaphor is the church as God's organization. Churches have officers such as elders, deacons, and others, and some of the leaders and administrators are to direct the affairs of their church. This is the business side of the church. While many of us don't like to acknowledge that the church has a business side, nonetheless it's true."

	The Church as Cause	The Church as Corporation
Metaphor	God's army fighting the good fight Romans 7:23; Ephesians 6:10–18; Philippians 2:25; 1 Timothy 1:18; 6:12; 2 Timothy 2:3–4	God's organization 1 Corinthians 12:12–31; 14:33, 37, 40; Philippians 2:25; Colossians 2:5; 1 Timothy 5:17
Emphasis	Leadership Romans 12:8	Administration 1 Corinthians 12:28
Focus	Outward	Inward
Role of Christ	Commanding Officer 2 Timothy 2:3–4	Head (authority) Matthew 28:18; 1 Corinthians 11:3
Role of the pastor	Leader and fellow soldier 1 Timothy 1:18	Administrator 1 Timothy 5:17
Role of the people	Soldiers 2 Timothy 2:4	Workers 1 Corinthians 3:9; 2 Timothy 2:15
Primary emotion	Excitement	Peace 1 Corinthians 14:33
Condition of the church in its absence	Directionless	Confusion

"The emphasis here is on the administrative aspect of the ministry. Leaders are to conduct the affairs of the church in a 'fitting and orderly way.' This involves developing strategic plans, implementing those plans, designing job descriptions, hiring staff, conducting meetings, developing budgets, evaluating performance, resolving conflicts, doing follow-up, and many other administrative aspects of the church. In addition most churches will incorporate to protect the assets of their staff and board against lawsuits. They will need to hire attorneys when entering into legal contracts that involve the purchase of land or the construction or renovation of their facilities.

"The obvious focus is inward. While an inward focus sounds bad, in at least two dimensions—the church as an organization and a community—it's necessary. To ignore this side of the church results in administrative chaos and potential lawsuits.

"Several roles are apparent with this organizational metaphor. Christ is at the head of the organization because the Father has given him all the authority to direct the affairs of his church. The elders or pastors work in the churches not only as leaders but capable, gifted administrators, conducting the affairs of the church. The people are the workers whom Christ has gifted. They, in turn, use their gifts to equip other workers to carry out the ministry of the church.

"The primary emotion people sense in a well-organized and administered church is peace, as opposed to disorder and confusion. The church conducts its ministries as well as all its affairs in a coordinated, well-ordered fashion.

"In my church, we decided to represent the corporate dimension like this." Again Steve drew a diagram at the bottom of the chart.

"Christ is the head of our organization," Steve explained, "and has all authority. All who fall below him on the chart are under his authority and accountable to him. The same is true for each group or person as you work your way down the structure. Next comes the congregation. This is because my church is congregational in its polity. Churches with a different polity might place the congregation elsewhere. Regardless, the church is under Christ's authority and accountable to him. The board is under the congregation's authority and accountable to them. Next comes the senior pastor who is under the board's authority. They have the authority to hire and fire me and they are also responsible to hold me accountable for my leadership of them and the rest of the congregation. Finally, I have authority over the staff. They function under my direction and are accountable to me. Should there be a problem at the staff level, the board and congregation look to me to deal with it. If the staff foul up, I share some responsibility."

Corporation

Christ

|

Congregation

|

Board

|

Pastor

|

Staff

"I can see how this structure would be an asset from a legal standpoint," Bob broke in.

"Exactly. Like most churches, Northpoint is incorporated under the laws of our state. Consequently if someone is injured on the church grounds, that person can sue the church but not the board, pastor, or staff. He or she would have to bring suit against the congregation for its assets as a whole. Again, the corporate structure reflects this, because the congregation precedes the board, pastor, and staff."

The Church as Community

Steve again handed Bob a chart. "One last chart," he said.

	The Church as Cause	The Church as Organization	The Church as Community
Metaphor	God's army fighting the good fight Romans 7:23; Ephesians 6:10–18; Philippians 2:25; 1 Timothy 1:18; 6:12; 2 Timothy 2:3–4	God's organization 1 Corinthians 12:12–31; 14:33, 37, 40; Philippians 2:25; Colossians 2:5; 1 Timothy 5:17	God's family Acts 2:44–46; Galations 3:28; 4:32, 34–36; Philippians 2:25; Hebrews 2:11–13
Emphasis	Leadership Romans 12:8	Administration 1 Corinthians 12:28	Relationship Ephesians 4:11–13
Focus	Outward	Inward	Inward
Role of Christ	Commanding Officer 2 Timothy 2:3–4	Head (authority) Matthew 28:18; 1 Corinthians 11:3	Brother Hebrews 2:11–13
Role of the pastor	Leader and fellow soldier 1 Timothy 1:18	Administrator 1 Timothy 5:17	Brother Hebrews 2:11–13
Role of the people	Soldiers 2 Timothy 2:4	Workers 1 Corinthians 3:9; 2 Timothy 2:15	Family 1 Timothy 5:1–2
Primary emotion	Excitement	Peace 1 Corinthians 14:33	Love Romans 13:8; 1 Peter 1:22; 1 John 3:11, 23; 4:7, 11–12; 2 John 5
Condition of the church in its absence	Directionless	Confusion	Sterility

The Dynamics of Church Leadership

"The third dimension is community. The metaphor is the church as God's family, caring for and treating one another as parents, siblings, and children. Hebrews 2:11–13 describes God's family as brothers, including Christ. At the same time, we are all equal in Christ. All the 'one another' passages in the New Testament explain the different ways that the family accomplishes community. Examples of community are found in Acts 2:44–46 and Acts 4:32, 34–35 where the early church as a family shared their possessions and sold them to help care for one another and meet one another's needs."

"In Philippians 2:25 doesn't Paul refer to Epaphroditus functioning in all three roles, as brother, fellow worker, and soldier?" Bob asked.

"I hadn't seen that passage. Thanks for pointing it out to me," Steve responded.

"The obvious emphasis of community is relationship," Steve said, pointing to the second row of the chart. "This is a necessary inward focus that attracts many people to seek out and join a church. Our church seeks to accomplish community through our many small-group ministries where people love and are loved, encourage and are encouraged, minister and are ministered to, care and are cared for, and admonish and are admonished. The roles are different from the cause and corporation dimensions. Christ, the pastor, the board, and the congregation relate to one another as brothers.

"Although numerous emotions surface in a family relationship, a primary emphasis of the community and the 'one another' passages is love. They can all be summed up under love: 'Love one another.'

"The absence of community in a church will prove devastating. Lost people as well as Christians desire authentic community and are looking everywhere for it. This probably has much to do with the breakdown of the family. A church that fails to provide a family atmosphere for its people and others creates a sterile environment that will result in its eventual death."

Steve drew another diagram. "The structure for community is entirely different from that for cause and corporation. The other structures are vertical, but community is horizontal.

Community

Christ —— Congregation —— Board —— Pastor —— Staff

"One key passage for this structure is Galatians 3:28 where Paul teaches about our unity and equality in Christ. The other is Hebrews 2:11–13 where the writer describes Christ and his people as brothers. The relationship is one of deeply caring for each other as family and risking vulnerability in a safe environment.

"I find it interesting that organizations in the marketplace are discovering the importance of the horizontal structure in relating better to their people and customers. The problem, however, is that at the same time, they are abandoning the vertical structure and remaining one-dimensional. This will create problems that only the vertical structure can solve."

"So you're saying that all organizations need both vertical and horizontal structures?" Bob asked.

"Yes, people in an organization will ask such questions as, 'To whom do I report and for whom am I responsible?' Organizations are multidimensional, needing both the vertical and horizontal structures."

The Relationships of the Church

"And you're saying that having these structures will help establish good relationships among the people in an organization—like me and my board?" Bob sighed as his thoughts were drawn back to his own situation.

"Yes, because with these structures in place, everyone knows where he or she fits into the picture and what his or her responsibilities are. Let's look at the relationship between pastors and their congregation, staff, and board."

The Pastor's Relationship to the Congregation, Staff, and Board

"Look at that last chart, at the role of the pastor."

"Yes, leader, manager, and brother," Bob read.

"Why don't you write those three terms across your sheet of paper. These are the pastor's core roles. Now, vertically on the left-hand side write the groups of people that pastors relate to frequently. The first is staff. I'm aware that some small churches have few if any staff, such as a part-time secretary or youth director. However, staff can and should include lay help. No pastor should operate without recruiting and developing some staff people, whether paid or voluntary. Next, write *the board*. They are the elders, deacons, trustees, and any others in positions of authority. And the third is the congregation. This covers everyone else in the church, including volunteer workers and active and inactive laypeople."

Bob wrote what Steve had directed, creating the beginnings of a chart.

The Pastor as Leader

Then Steve drew an imaginary line with his finger on Bob's paper. "The place where the pastor's roles and the groups intersect is where you write the kind of relationship they have. The pastor as leader relates to the congregation, staff, and board as a primary influencer. Remember that an important part of my definition of leaders or leadership is influence. Each group is to look to the pastor to cast the vision, to clarify the cause, and to challenge them as fellow soldiers to charge the hill and rout the forces of the world, the flesh, and the devil. The pastor uses his influence to accomplish the church's mission—the Great Commission—and to make a difference in the lives of lost and saved people."

"That's exciting," Bob said, smiling and shaking his head.

The Pastor as Administrator

"Next, as an administrator the pastor relates differently to each group. With the staff, he's their employer. He is responsible for them, and they are responsible to him because they are under his authority."

"He's the boss!" Bob offered.

"Not exactly. That's a little strong for his role. While he does give direction, he's also a servant who is responsible to see that the staff are best using their abilities to serve the church."

"I understand," Bob said. "So you're saying I should stop giving orders?"

Steve chuckled and went on. "When it comes to the board, at my church, I as pastor am an employee who is accountable to and answers to the board. And because our church has a congregational polity, I am also the congregation's employee. (Churches with a different polity would relate differently here.) I'm answerable to the congregation through the board."

The Pastor as Brother

"Finally, the pastor as a brother relates to all three groups as a caregiver who seeks to help them meet their spiritual and emotional needs in the context of our community groups. Consequently, though the pastor may not directly care for all the people in the church—that would be impossible—he is responsible to see that the mechanisms are in place so that people are cared for as family."

When Bob had finished writing, he had produced the following chart.

The Pastor's Roles

	Leader	Administrator	Brother
Staff	Influencer	Employer	Caregiver
Board	Influencer	Employee	Caregiver
Congregation	Influencer	Employee (depending on polity)	Caregiver

The Need to Clarify the Relationships

"This chart is great. I can take one look and see where I'm not relating well to the people in my church. For example, I can see where the breakdown occurred between me, my administrative assistant, and the board member. She was wrong in going over my head to the board member. As my employee, she should have come to me first. And the board member, as my employer, should have come to me first before raising it as an issue at the board meeting. He also should have directed the staff member to me before listening to her complaint."

"Yes, they were both at serious fault. However, I believe that to a lesser extent, you're at fault as well," cautioned Steve.

Bob's eyebrows shot up. "What do you mean?"

"You're guilty of assuming that everyone understood these relationships and where you draw the lines."

"That's true," Bob had to agree.

"I made the same mistake when I first arrived at my church," Steve admitted. "It was only a matter of time before a disagreement occurred that surfaced the need to draw these lines of demarcation.

"Another matter that's important to your relationship with your people is that they know which hat you're wearing when you relate to them," Steve continued. "For example, a staff member, such as an administrative assistant, may not be performing up to expectation. You will need to sit down with that person and discuss the matter. The question is, Which hat will you wear? Will you relate to him or her as administrator or brother? At different times you may relate in different ways. At first, you may come alongside the person as a caring brother, probing the problem and seeking a mutual solution that benefits him or her as well as the church. However, if the individual proves incompetent or does nothing to improve, you'll need to put on the administrator's hat and strongly warn him or her or even release the person. I would go so far as to say that you might want to say which hat you're wearing as you relate to your staff. I've had to do this on several occasions when someone wasn't getting it.

"One final point," Steve said, glancing at his watch. "Neither you nor I will be good at all three relational roles—leader, administrator, brother. For example, you may be good as an influencer and caregiver, but not so good as an employer. That's understood because it's rare that one person is skilled in all three areas. My advice is to be aware of your strong areas and your limitations. Focus on your strengths and get help from gifted people where you're limited."

After praying together the two men stood at the same time. Steve walked Bob to the door. "I didn't even ask if you got started on developing your mission."

Bob frowned. "That's another long story!"

"Oh? Did anything we said today help with how to proceed?"

"Yes, actually, I think it did," Bob said, looking hopeful. "I think I need to approach the board as a caregiver (which I think is my strength) rather than just trying to be an influencer."

"Sounds like a good insight," Steve said. "Let me know next week how it goes."

The terms *cause, corporation,* and *community* aren't original with me. Though I don't necessarily use them in the same way, I got them from my friend and former classmate Jim Dethmer, "Moving in the Right Circles," *Leadership* (fall 1992): 86–91.

For Scripture relating to the church's purpose, see Romans 15:16; 1 Corinthians 6:20; to its mission, see Matthew 28:19–20; Mark 16:1; to the building of Christ's church, see Matthew 16:18.

Concerning the horizontal structure and the marketplace, see James A. Belasco and Ralph C. Stayer, *Flight of the Buffalo* (New York: Warner, 1993).

Five

Pastors and Change
Developing a Theology of Change

"After last week's session on relating to my congregation, staff, and board, I've begun to pay more attention to how I relate to people. I find it difficult to be an influencer and not a pusher, which seems to be my tendency because I don't feel comfortable in the role. I keep reminding myself that people are more important than getting stuff done." Bob and Steve were standing by the coffeepot, fixing their coffee, before beginning their sixth session together.

"Yes," Steve agreed, "if people matter to God, then they must matter to us. So did you make any progress on your mission?"

"I'd say so." Bob hesitated, added more sugar to his coffee, and took a sip. "I've thought a lot about it and would like you to take a look at some of my ideas." Steve nodded and waited for Bob to go on. "I guess I've decided to move slowly with the board. I don't want them to think I've come in to change everything. When I first mentioned the idea of developing a mission and strategy, they seemed to go on the defensive and began talking about the past and all they've done."

"That's not an unusual reaction," Steve said. "And it does have to do with change and the fear of it. But change happens, whether we like it or not. It's a constant in the twenty-first century and it affects the church as well as the rest of society, so we need to prepare for it. We're going to talk about this today. I hope our discussion will give you some ideas of how to move your church forward.

"You know," Steve continued, "change in our society is like a whirling vortex that can swallow up churches as well as other organizations that don't know how to deal with it. I believe that a major reason why 80 to 85 percent of the churches in North America are plateaued or in decline is because they don't know how to deal with spiraling, complex change. Many are afraid of change, and their response to it is to become passive. Someone in the church—often the board but sometimes the pastor—bugles a retreat and everyone falls back.

"More change has taken place in the latter half of the twentieth century and the beginning of the twenty-first century than has occurred since the founding of this nation. Currently we are experiencing a major transformation that is rearranging society—its worldview, basic values, social and political structures, arts, and key institutions. Soon a whole new world—the postmodern world—will exist that will be different from the world that you and I grew up in."

"It's true," Bob broke in. "It's hard to believe all the technological advances, to say nothing of the way people are changing. But haven't churches throughout history had to deal with change? That certainly comes across in the Book of Acts and has been my impression from my reading of church history."

Steve nodded. "Yes, that's why I contend that the church has always needed a theology of change, and this need will only increase in the future. The tragedy is that few seem to have addressed the issue.

"I argue that we must be active and aggressive when it comes to handling change in our churches. That's one of the reasons why you experienced two services—one contemporary and one traditional—on Sunday morning when you and your wife visited my church. However, you can't be active and aggressive unless you have a theology of change that's true to the Bible and will guide you through the change process. My goal for today's session is to present and explore my theology of change with you. You can probe it and see if it has any soft spots."

"Humph. That's unlikely." Bob grinned. "You've thought all this stuff through pretty well, I'd say!"

Steve went on. "Every Christian institution, whether it's a church or parachurch ministry, has to wrestle with the vexing question, What must and must not change? To answer this question for our churches, those of us who lead them in the twenty-first century must develop a theology of change. My theology of change consists of three Fs: function, form, and freedom."

"Interesting," Bob said. "What exactly do you mean by function?"

Function

"I want to give you my definition," Steve said. "Ready?"

The Definition of Functions

Bob turned over several pages of notes until he came to a clean sheet, then, ready to write, he looked at Steve.

"I define the functions of the church as the timeless, unchanging, nonnegotiable precepts that are based on Scripture and are mandates for all churches to pursue to accomplish their purpose."

Bob asked Steve to repeat the definition as he wrote it down.

Functions are the timeless, unchanging, nonnegotiable precepts that are based on Scripture and are mandates for all churches to pursue to accomplish their purpose.

Characteristics

"I need to clarify some of this," Steve said. "Let's begin with some of the characteristics of functions that make them absolutes. First, they are timeless. As long as there's a church, they must be present. They were true of Christ's church in the first century, they'll continue to be true of his church in the twenty-first century, and they'll be true as long as the church remains on earth. For example, evangelism, as a function, characterized the first-century church and it should characterize twenty-first-century churches as well.

"Second, functions are unchanging. God doesn't make evangelism or worship functions of the first-century church and then change them for the twentieth- or twenty-first-century church. Christ instituted certain functions for his church at Pentecost that will remain the same until he takes his church home.

Consequently it doesn't matter how much change sweeps across the church. It must not abandon these functions. They're here to stay.

"Third, the functions are nonnegotiable. As churches of the first century couldn't pick and choose the functions they would observe or ignore, neither can the church in the twenty-first century. A number of churches in North America are what I call 'niche churches.'"

"What do you mean by that?" Bob asked.

"A niche church is a church that's known for a particular ministry strength. For instance, in several of the larger cities in the Bible Belt, some churches are strong in the areas of family ministries and children's programs. Some are strong in counseling. Others are known for their preaching and teaching the Bible or their worship. Though churches will have certain strengths, Christ has commanded all churches to make disciples—not to make niches. A church's success is based on its disciples, not its niches."

"So you think they're wrong?" asked Bob.

"Yes, and my beef is that in so many of them evangelism is extremely weak or nonexistent," Steve frowned as he thought about his concern. "They've unconsciously negotiated evangelism away for some other function, such as worship or teaching, and that contradicts Christ's Great Commission."

"That's a really good point," Bob said. "I never thought about it like that."

Basis

"Well," Steve answered, "I'm basing all of this on what I see in Scripture. And Scripture is the basis or foundation for all the functions of the church. We find the functions in the Bible; therefore, they must be biblical." Steve opened his Bible to 2 Timothy 3:16–17, which he read: "'All Scripture is God-breathed and is useful for teaching, rebuking, correcting and training in righteousness, so that the man of God may be thoroughly equipped for every good work.' We find the functions in such descriptive passages as Acts 2:42–47; 4:35; and 6:4. But there are also prescriptive passages. First Timothy 4:13; 1 Corinthians 11:23–26; and Colossians 4:1–2 (among others) tell the church certain things that must be done."

Usage

"So these timeless functions serve as mandates for the church," Bob said.

"Yes, since they are timeless, unchanging, and are based on the Bible, they comprise the church's ministry precepts. If you want to know what your church should be doing and what you have in common with the churches of the first century, discover the church's functions. They are absolutes that are to be a part of every church's ministry."

Implication

"What you're saying, then," Bob broke in again, "is that all churches must pursue these functions and not just their particular ministry niche."

"That's right." Steve agreed. "If a church is weak in evangelism and strong in Bible teaching, then it needs to work hard at becoming stronger in its evangelistic efforts. If it's weak in good Bible teaching but strong in worship or evangelism, then it needs to shore up its Bible teaching."

"Sounds as if it would be wise for churches such as mine to make a list of their functions and then evaluate how they're doing."

"Yes," Steve nodded, "but few ever do."

Purpose

"Finally, the church's functions serve a purpose. Functions such as fellowship, evangelism, and worship all work together to accomplish the church's overall purpose—to glorify God."

Bob had made a chart of the information Steve had given him on functions.

Functions

Characteristics	timeless, unchanging, nonnegotiable precepts (absolute)
Basis	based on Scripture
Usage	mandates (ministry precepts)
Implication	all churches must pursue (found in the Bible)
Purpose	accomplish the church's overall purpose

Some Examples of Functions

"Can you give me some examples of functions?" Bob asked. "I've always found that examples are helpful in understanding concepts."

Basic functions

"Sure. I mentioned the Acts 2:42–47 passage, and, while it isn't exhaustive, I believe that it describes several basic functions that all churches share in common and that are prescribed in other parts of the New Testament. They are teaching, fellowship, prayer, care, worship, and evangelism."

Organization

Steve continued as Bob was writing down the list. "A function that I've heard few churches mention is found in 1 Corinthians 14:33, 40 and Colossians 2:5. We looked at these last time, where Paul is teaching the important function of organization. I'll read 1 Corinthians 14:40: 'But everything should be done in a fitting and orderly way.' Paul commends the church at Colossae because it's organized and orderly."

Ordinances

"The ordinances are also legitimate functions of the church. Though different denominations and organizations may debate their forms, most agree that baptism—our identification with Christ as believers—and the Lord's Supper—our remembrance of Christ—are primary, critical functions of the church."

Bob had completed his list of church functions and looked it over.

Common Functions

Teaching	Evangelism
Fellowship	Organization
Prayer	Baptism
Care	Lord's Supper
Worship	

The Discovery of Functions

"How can you know what is and isn't a function?" Bob asked. "And how did you know what to include on your list? How do you discover the church's functions?"

"In two ways," Steve explained. "First, functions are ends, not means to ends. Second, they explain why the church does what it does. So whenever I'm not sure if a concept is a function, I ask two questions: Is it an end, as opposed to a means to an end? and Why are we doing it? Actually, all the functions do have a common end that I included in my definition. It's to glorify God. But that's not what I'm talking about here.

"Let's revisit some of the examples I gave you. One is prayer. Prayer is talking to God. The question becomes, Is prayer an end in itself? If it means talking to God, then the answer is yes. Let's ask the other question, Why do we pray? The answer is to talk to God. So I feel that prayer should be considered one of the church's functions. Another is evangelism. Evangelism involves both telling about and entering into an eternal relationship with God through faith in Christ. That's an end—something we are called to accomplish—and it answers the question, Why do we evangelize? So it is a function of the church. I have much more to say about the discovery of functions but I'll wait until I discuss the concept of form. Then we'll explore it further."

Form

"Do you have a definition of *form* for me?" Bob asked.

The Definition of Forms

"Yes, forms are the temporal, changing, negotiable practices that are based on culture and are methods that all churches are free to choose to accomplish their functions."

"You'll need to repeat that," Bob said. He had stopped writing, not able to remember the end of the definition.

Forms are the temporal, changing, negotiable practices that are based

*on culture and are methods that all
churches are free to choose to
accomplish their functions.*

Characteristics

Steve continued when Bob was ready. "The characteristics of the forms are the opposite of those of the functions. That makes them nonabsolutes. They have three characteristics. First, the forms are temporal or timely. The ones that the first-century church used in ministry may or may not be the same as those the church in the twenty-first century uses. The question is, What practices and forms best serve our constituency or the people we desire to reach?

"Second, forms are changing. The functions are unchanging, but I would go so far as to say that the forms *must* change. This is where change takes place in the church. As leaders, we pastors can learn from the men of Issachar, 'who understood the times and knew what Israel should do.' That's 1 Chronicles 12:32. Times change and so must our forms of ministry if the church is to remain culturally current. So functions never change, but forms must change.

"And third, the forms are negotiable, unlike the functions that are nonnegotiable. We can pick and choose the forms that are best for our church. When they've served their usefulness, we choose new ones. In my church, traditional worship primarily reached the older generation of members. However, I've negotiated a second service that uses a more contemporary form of worship that will enable us to reach the younger generation, who up to now were dropping out after they completed high school."

"What's interesting," Bob broke in, "is that the liberal churches have reversed function and form."

"What do you mean?" Steve asked.

"The liberal churches have treated the functions as temporal, changing, and negotiable, but the forms as timeless, unchanging, and practically nonnegotiable. On the one hand, they've abandoned the faith of the Bible in their attempt to be relevant to modern times. On the other hand, they've clung to old practices that seem to be losing their effectiveness. They lose on both counts."

"That's a good observation," Steve said. "And they've suffered for it. The mainline denominations experienced their greatest loss of people during the second half of the twentieth century. And I think you've identified part of the reason for that loss."

Basis

"Now concerning the basis for forms, whereas the basis for the church's functions is the Scriptures, the basis for its forms is culture. If our churches are going to reach the people of this culture, then they need to understand the culture. I'll say more about this in our session next week on culture. The typical Christian has been taught that anything that has to do with culture is automatically bad. That's simply not the case and it's a position that doesn't square with Scripture. Culture isn't all bad.

"The church expresses its truths through cultural forms. My argument is that those cultural forms should be understandable and make reasonable sense to those to whom we minister or else we won't communicate."

"That's certainly true on the mission field," Bob added, "and North America has become a mission field."

Usage

"The functions serve as mandates for the church, and the forms serve as methods. They are methods through which the church accomplishes its functions. On the one hand, worship is a function. On the other hand, a contemporary worship format is a ministry practice or method. The same is true of a traditional format. That's why it's okay to change a church's worship format, because it's a means to an end, and not the end. As long as you don't jettison the function of worship, you're free biblically to change how you do worship."

Bob sighed, "Yes, but you should make sure that the rest of the church agrees with your change."

"That goes without saying. My point is that many people have believed that a contemporary format, using guitars and drums for instance, is wrong. Some even believe it is unbiblical but it's not."

Bob was adding a column on forms to the chart he had already made. "Is the implication of forms next?" he asked.

Implication

Steve chuckled. "Yes. The church's functions are absolutes based on Scripture that serve as mandates for a church's ministry. Thus the implication is that all churches must pursue them rather than some specialty niche. But since the church's forms are nonabsolutes based on culture and serve as methods for its ministry, the implication is that all churches are free to choose the ones that work best for them in conducting their ministry. This freedom is to be mixed with wisdom, however. What a church is free to do and what is wise may not always be the same. I'll say more about freedom later."

Purpose

"Now, concerning the forms' purpose. I said earlier that a church's functions exist to accomplish the church's purpose, which is to honor or glorify God. The church's forms exist to accomplish the church's functions. You've heard it said, 'Form follows function.' I would say form serves function. Remember in 1 Corinthians 9:22 how Paul said, 'To the weak I became weak, to win the weak. I have become all things to all men so that by all possible means I might save some'? His goal was to win people to Christ (a function) and he would do it by whatever means necessary. When functions are in the driver's seat—where they should be—the church identifies its functions and then repeatedly asks, What forms best accomplish each function? Since one of the functions is evangelism, the church asks, How can we best reach lost people? The answer is the various forms or methods for evangelism.

"It's important to remember that these forms will and should change as the culture changes. While various methods are not bad in themselves, after a little time they may have served their usefulness. That's what I call 'shelf life.' Then it's time to choose another more effective method. The tendency of the typical church, however, is to equate its functions with the cultural forms it uses to accomplish them."

"I think that's where my church is," Bob said. "They think the only way to do things is the way they've been doing them since the church opened its doors."

"When a church confuses form with function, change becomes difficult if not impossible and the church begins to decline. The answer to this problem is for pastors like you and me to teach on this topic and to train our churches to hold their forms with an open hand. A program of regular church evaluation will help churches accomplish this objective because one of the things that a good audit evaluates is the church's methods."

As Steve finished speaking, Bob completed the second column of his chart.

	Functions	Forms
Characteristics	timeless, unchanging, nonnegotiable precepts (absolute)	temporal, changing, negotiable (relative)
Basis	based on Scripture	based on culture
Usage	mandates (ministry precepts)	methods (ministry practices)
Implication	all churches must pursue (found in the Bible)	all churches are free to choose (agree with the Bible)
Purpose	accomplish the church's overall purpose	accomplish the church's functions

Some Examples of Forms

"I think I understand forms," Bob said, "especially when you contrast forms with functions. But how about some examples."

"Okay. Let's use the same three categories we did for functions and match them with certain forms."

Basic Forms

"We noted earlier in Acts 2:42–47 that the Jerusalem church had devoted itself to a number of functions: teaching, fellowship, prayer, care, worship, and evangelism. For each of these functions, a number of forms exist to accomplish them.

"Let's focus again on evangelism. Over the years, churches have developed a number of methods or forms for carrying out evangelism. In the New Testament Peter in particular preached several evangelistic messages that resulted in many people coming to the Savior. Early in the twentieth century, evangelists such as Billy Sunday, D. L. Moody, and Billy Graham used their gifts to conduct evangelistic crusades.

"Another form of evangelism is confrontational. It involves going door-to-door or confronting people in public places with the gospel. A third form is friendship evangelism that emphasizes the importance of building relationships with people before sharing the gospel with them. Then there is the approach developed by the Coral Ridge Presbyterian Church in Fort Lauderdale, Florida, that combines confrontation and friendship evangelism, called Evangelism Explosion.

"We find at the beginning of the twenty-first century, however, that some of these forms or methods are not as effective as they once were, especially in reaching new, younger generations of North Americans. Thus God is using other methods of evangelism. One such method is found in Pastor Steve Sjogren's book *Conspiracy of Kindness*. He and his church are implementing a form of evangelism that involves them in doing deeds of kindness for unbelievers, expecting and accepting nothing in return. This method of evangelism is most helpful because anyone in the church can do a deed of kindness for another, such as mowing a neighbor's yard, washing a car at a free church-sponsored car wash, painting a house, carrying a sack of groceries, giving away free beverages, and so on."

"I've heard of that method," Bob said. "It sounds like it would be effective. Almost everyone likes free help!" They both laughed.

"The arrival of the Information Age and the rapid development of information technology surrounding the computer may open up a new frontier for doing evangelism," Steve continued. "For example, as the Internet has come on-line, some churches are developing evangelistic web sites."

Bob had made a list of the evangelistic forms Steve mentioned.

Evangelistic Forms

Function	Forms
Evangelism	Crusades
	Door-to-door
	Friendships
	Deeds of kindness
	Web sites

Organization

"As I said earlier, another function that Paul emphasizes in 1 Corinthians 14:33 and 40 and Colossians 2:5 is organization. The question is, What forms implement or accomplish organization? The answer is polity or church government. Paul is arguing in 1 Corinthians and Colossians for organization or church government. Over the years, churches have settled on three basic forms: episcopal, presbyterian, and congregational."

"Is one of those forms any more biblical than the others?" Bob asked.

"That's a good question. Those who believe in church government by bishops use such passages as Acts 15:13–21 where James exercises great authority to argue for his position. Churches that have opted for the presbyterian form use the elders' role in the Jerusalem council in Acts 15:1–35, along with passages such as 1 Timothy 3:4–5 and 5:17. Churches that argue for congregational rule use Acts 6:3–5; 15:12, 22–23, 25, and doctrines such as the priesthood of the believer."

"And since we're talking about organizational form, we're free to choose the one we want, correct?"

"Yes." Steve agreed. "My view is that all three are valid forms that churches may employ. The issue is which form best serves the church's purpose at this point in its development. Some people falsely assume that all the early churches used a single best form and only that form. But this is an argument from silence."

Again, Bob had made a list in his notes.

Organizational Forms

Function	Forms
Organization	Episcopal
	Presbyterian
	Congregational

Ordinances

"We know that the ordinances of baptism and the Lord's Supper are important functions of the church. I believe that there are several different and legitimate forms for accomplishing these functions.

"As you know, over the centuries, immersion, sprinkling, and pouring have been the accepted traditional forms of baptism. Many contend that immersion is the biblically correct form, arguing that it was the common practice throughout Christendom."

"That's not a strong argument is it?" asked Bob.

"No, it isn't. Certainly immersion best pictures the significance of baptism. That's why I immerse new believers at my church."

"So do I—for the same reason."

"However, that argument isn't strong enough to disallow the other modes as legitimate baptisms, especially in situations where one can't be immersed, such as sickness or lack of enough water.

"I've heard pastors debate," Steve continued, "what the proper elements of the Lord's Supper are. Some argue that when Christ instituted the Supper, it was at the time of the Passover; therefore, he must have used unleavened bread that would be equivalent to today's matzo."

"But the passage isn't prescriptive, is it?" Bob questioned.

"No, it's not," Steve said. "The Savior commanded that his church observe the Supper in rememberance of him but he didn't command that we use unleavened bread. Nor did he say what we should drink. The passage doesn't command that we use wine or grape juice or some kind of unfermented wine. In our church we use grape juice because a number of our people, especially some of our new believers, are recovering alcoholics."

"We use grape juice as well," added Bob, "but it's more from tradition than anything else."

The phone rang as Steve and Bob were finishing their discussion of the ordinances. Steve answered it and Bob used the time to make a list of forms of the ordinances.

Forms of the Ordinances

Function	Forms
Baptism	Immersion, Sprinkling, Pouring
Lord's Supper	Wine, Grape juice, Matzo Bread, Crackers

The Discovery of Forms

"That was my secretary," Steve said, "reminding me of my next appointment. I have to be at the home of one of my deacons in forty-five minutes."

"Should we stop here?" Bob asked.

"No, let's try to finish. Then we can start right in on culture next time. I just want to say a few words about discovering forms.

"People often ask how we can know what are forms and what are functions. In some cases, it's easy to tell them apart; in others, it's not so easy. Remember when we were talking about discovering the church's functions, we used two questions: Is it an end as opposed to a means? and Why do you do what you do? There are two similar questions that help us discover the church's forms: Is it a means to an end? and How do you do what you do? or How will you implement a particular function?

"Let me give you some examples. Baptism is a function because it represents our identity with Christ. But how do you know this? The answer is that it symbolizes identity with Christ, and that makes it an end in itself. That's its meaning. However, the various forms or modes of baptism (immersion and so forth) aren't ends but means to an end. For instance, we don't immerse people simply to be immersing them. That would make immersion an end in itself. Immersion as well as other forms are means to the end—identification with Christ (the meaning of baptism).

"The second question is, How do you baptize people? The answer is the form, such as immersion, sprinkling, pouring, or whatever form you and your denomination accepts.

"Let's consider teaching biblical truth, such as teaching the apostles' doctrine in Acts 2:42. The meaning of teaching in this context is the communication of biblical truth. That's a legitimate end in itself. However, several forms of teaching exist that are the means to this end. One is the public lecture as in a church service or some Bible classes. Another is teaching through dialogue where different people teach and there's much interaction. Both are answers to the question, How will you teach?"

Steve glanced at his watch, decided they had time to finish up his theology of change, and continued.

Freedom

"The third of the three Fs in my theology of change is freedom."

"I'm glad we have time for this," Bob said. "I'm curious how freedom fits into your theology."

Implications

Steve smiled as he opened his Bible to James. "In two places James clearly states that the Bible, which he calls the 'perfect law,' gives us freedom. That's in James 1:25 and 2:12. This certainly applies to the area of form, since churches are free to choose the form to accomplish the function. All churches under the guidance of the Holy Spirit are free to choose the forms or methods that they find best accomplish the functions. Because the forms are nonabsolutes, each church has vast freedom in how they do church."

"Okay. I can see that." Bob nodded.

Limitations

"We limit our own freedom, however, when we assume that there is only one correct way to implement a concept, such as church government or polity. For example, when we discover the different views of the church's polity (episcopal, presbyterian, and congregational), we assume that only one is the correct view and begin to look for it. Initially that's okay. However, after investigating the biblical evidence, if we find that there isn't only one correct view, then we must be open to the idea that these are forms and that several different forms are legitimate. And we have freedom with nonabsolutes to use the form we find appropriate."

Restrictions

"I can think of only two restrictions that affect our freedom to choose forms. Forms must agree with the Bible. That means that while they may not be found in the Bible, the forms must not contradict or disagree in any way with the teaching of the Bible. That's how we know that the Holy Spirit is involved. The New Testament sets the boundary, and each local church is free under the Holy Spirit to minister within that boundary. The second restriction is that our forms—whatever the function (worship, teaching, evangelism, and so on)—must help us accomplish those absolutes and grow in Christ. When this ceases to happen, it becomes imperative that we look for and embrace other more workable forms.

"There's a great quote from Francis Schaeffer that speaks to what we've been saying about change." Steve read, "'Not being able, as times change, to change under the Holy Spirit is ugly. The same applies to church polity and practice. In a rapidly changing age like ours, an age of total upheaval like ours, to make nonabsolutes absolutes guarantees both isolation and the death of the institutional, organized church.'"

After prayer both men rushed to their cars, hoping not to be too late for their next appointment.

The theology of change presented in this chapter is part of a bigger picture that comprises hermeneutics. To some degree, ministry is hermeneutics. Pastors need to determine what they can and can't do in their church. The answer is found in a good hermeneutic for "doing" church. I recommend that all pastors read my book *Doing Church: A Biblical Guide for Leading Ministries through Change* (Grand Rapids: Kregel, 1999), which covers the information in this chapter in greater depth. It's the only book I know of that helps pastors think through what their church can and can't do according to Scripture.

The purpose of the church is to glorify God, found in Romans 15:16; 1 Corinthians 6:20; 10:31; 1 Timothy 1:17.

References for the church ordinances are Romans 6:3–5 (baptism) and 1 Corinthians 11:23–26 (Lord's Supper).

Peter's evangelistic messages are found in Acts 2:14–41; 3:11–4:4.

For Pastor Steve Sjogren's method of evangelism, see his book *Conspiracy of Kindness* (Ann Arbor, Mich.: Servant, 1993).

The doctrine of the priesthood of the believer is based on Hebrews 10:19–22; 1 Peter 2:5, 9.

The Francis Schaeffer quote comes from his book, *The Church at the End of the Twentieth Century* (Wheaton: Crossway, 1970), 68.

Pastors and Culture
Developing a Theology of Culture

Pastor Steve and Pastor Bob were getting together for their last session before summer. They had decided that in light of their hectic summer schedules, they should take a break until fall. Bob had found that the information and the encouragement Steve gave him each week had been invaluable, and he already felt that he was making progress in his relationships with his staff, board, and congregation. He was convinced, however, that he would benefit from more of Steve's mentoring, so he made sure that their sessions would begin again in September.

As they sat down together on this early morning that was beginning to feel a lot like summer, Bob thanked Steve for all he had done for him. "You've given me so much to work on, it's probably good that we aren't meeting again until September. This will give me time to implement what we've been covering in our sessions. I can apply some of the material such as that on change immediately. However, I'm still in the process of working with my church in discovering our values and developing a mission and a strategy. I hope that by the end of the summer I'll have something to show you."

"I'm sure you will. Once you get everyone moving in the same direction, the whole process goes pretty quickly." Steve glanced at the coffeepot. "I think the coffee's ready and I'm ready for one of those donuts you brought."

When they sat back down with their mugs of coffee and sugar donuts on napkins, Steve said, "Now let's talk theology of culture. I contend that early twenty-first-century churches must develop a theology of culture. You're probably thinking that's nothing new and you're correct. Ever since the church began on the day of Pentecost, it has needed a theology of culture, and this need will continue as long as the church exists on earth."

"I understand what you're saying but I'm not aware of any churches that have articulated a clear, coherent theology of culture," Bob said. "Of course, I hadn't even given it a thought until the last few weeks when you started talking about traditions, hermeneutics, and change."

"My experience is that most pastors, even when seminary trained, have never thought through a theology of culture. The people in their churches are even less likely to have given it any thought. While some have done so intuitively at an unconscious level, most haven't thought it through at a conscious level. However, as change sweeps over our churches, and we come into contact with more and different cultures, we will inevitably face practical issues and questions that only a biblical theology of culture can address. For example, How should we as Christians relate to culture? What is culture? What does the Bible say about culture? Is it a friend or an enemy of the church? The answers lie in one's theology of culture.

"We don't have time today to discuss a complete the-ology of culture. So let's briefly address five areas that will affect our thinking about culture. First, we must explore why culture is so important to us and our churches. Next, we need to define culture so that we know what we're talking about. Then we'll discuss how best to respond to culture. We'll explore the relation-ship between the gospel and culture. And finally, we'll address how the church should relate to culture."

"Wow, that sounds like a lot to cover in two hours, but I'm ready!" Bob said, pulling his pen out of his jacket pocket.

The Importance of Culture

"There are several reasons that culture is important to leaders and their churches. Culture profoundly shapes and influences all of our life and beliefs, and most of us aren't aware of it. We use culture to order our life, interpret our experiences, and evaluate behav-ior. Out of our culture and what we experience, we cre-ate our reality and make sense of our life. This is pretty much a mental reflex, an unconscious process. We're hardly aware that it's taking place. It simply happens.

"Another reason that culture is so important is that our cultural presuppositions affect the development of our theology and what we believe about the Bible. Our culture provides a semantic, conceptual frame-work through which we view God and the Bible. Most of us who are in ministry in evangelical pulpits have been educated under a western European influence. The institutions where we've trained were heavily influ-enced by a European system using European theolo-gians. It's very likely that Europeans wrote the various theologies you've read or the commentaries you've followed. We spent far more time in seminary studying the didactic or teaching books of the Bible than the narrative books. That's very western."

"Do you think that's bad?" Bob asked.

"While it's not bad," Steve answered, "it does reflect a theological viewpoint developed in the cauldron of a western European culture.

"A third reason why culture is important is that it affects the way we conduct our ministries in the church. Our own cultural context has shaped much of our practice of the faith as well as our understanding of the faith. From a cultural perspective, many of our older, traditional churches across North America were 'made in Europe,' whereas the new-paradigm churches were 'made in America.' For example, European-influenced churches view the church as a building that looks like a church with property. Their organization is hierarchical, they emphasize the role and training of the clergy, they're more formal in dress and worship, they focus more on the past, and their music was written before the 1960s. American-influenced churches view the church more as people. Their organization is more horizontal, they emphasize the role and training of the laity, they're more casual in dress and worship, their focus is on the future, and their music was written after 1960."

Bob smiled. "You're right! And guess where my church was made!"

"I know," Steve said. "And that's unfortunate. At the end of the twentieth century, the European-influenced churches have been in decline, while the American-influenced churches have been growing. In addition, a number of European-influenced churches have experienced a push by their younger people to transition to a more culturally current American-influenced format. This has usually been met with much resistance, and in some instances, churches have split over it. The problem is that some of these people in the European-influenced churches believe that they're defending the faith, not their cultural heritage. So they fight as if the entire future of orthodox Christianity depends on them."

Bob was shaking his head.

"A fourth reason that culture is important is that it helps us understand better the different people whom we seek to reach for Christ. We live at a time of growing cultural diversity. Consequently, as we reach out and minister to people with the gospel, it will be to an increasingly multicultural North America. This is happening both within and outside ethnic boundaries. For example, within ethnic boundaries, white Generation Xers live in and experience a different culture from white Baby Boomers. And both embrace a culture that's totally different from their white parents and grandparents. We shouldn't be too surprised when the younger generations fail to embrace the cultural aspects of their parents' and grandparents' Christianity. The same holds true in the African-American, Hispanic, Asian, and other communities.

"Outside ethnic boundaries, America has become a multicultural, global nation. North America isn't a melting pot any longer, it's a salad bowl. We commonly speak of Mexican Americans, African-Americans, and Asian Americans. And in some cities, one of these groups is the dominant racial group, not whites. Whereas once many North American companies conducted their business only in North America, now most have business interests around the world. Along with improved communication technology, this has brought us into contact with people from many different cultures. All this poses questions for the church, such as, How can we best reach these people for Christ?"

As Steve spoke, Bob was listing the reasons that culture is important. Here is what he wrote:

Reasons Why Culture Is Important

1. It profoundly shapes and influences all our life and beliefs.
2. It affects the development of our theology and what we believe about the Bible.
3. It affects the way we conduct our ministries in the church.
4. It helps us better understand the different people whom we seek to reach for Christ.

"So what exactly are we talking about when we speak of culture?" Bob asked.

The Definition of Culture

Steve spoke through the bite of donut in his mouth. "I do have a definition of culture. And often I find it helpful to talk about what culture isn't as well as what it is. That helps to further refine our thoughts. But let's begin by focusing on what culture is."

What Culture Is

Steve finished his donut, brushed his face with a napkin, and began. "Traditional definitions of culture usually include such elements as people's thoughts, beliefs, values, speech, actions, and artifacts. I view these elements as falling under people's beliefs and actions.

Therefore I define culture as the sum total of what people believe and how they act. It's the sum of a people's way of life, and it's largely through culture that people of different ethnic, social, or religious groups create and make sense of the world they live in."

Bob wrote the definition in his notes:

> *Culture is the sum total of what people believe and how they act.*

Beliefs

"I realize that my definition is broad," Steve continued, "so let's examine the two elements that make up the definition. First, culture includes people's beliefs. At the core of everyone's beliefs is a worldview. Your worldview consists of your answers to the basic questions of life, such as, What is real? Who are we? Where did we come from? Why are we here? What happens to us at death? What is the basis for morality and ethics? Your answers to these questions inform the assumptions that influence your total belief system. Some western worldviews are theism, deism, and modernism (naturalism). Currently we are in the midst of a shift from modernism to a new worldview—postmodernism. This view answers the above questions differently than all the former worldviews and will influence the thinking not only of the current generations but of those to come for the next one hundred years or so.

"Our worldview dictates what we think and believe is true. We hold our beliefs at two levels. At one level are our operating beliefs. They are the beliefs that we act on. These are beliefs that affect and influence our values and overall behavior. At another level are our theoretical beliefs. They are the beliefs that are held at a theoretical level and may or may not affect our life. A church's doctrinal statement or creed would be one example."

Actions

"Culture also consists of people's actions or human behavior. Our actions are affected by our beliefs and include what we say as well as how we act. What we say gets into language and communication. How we act involves what we do and the things we make. We have patterned ways of doing things, such as how we relate to people, our role in society and family, our vocation, where we go, what we read, and a host of other things. What we make involves material objects, such as clothing, tools, art, houses, and so forth."

Bob's notes on culture looked like this:

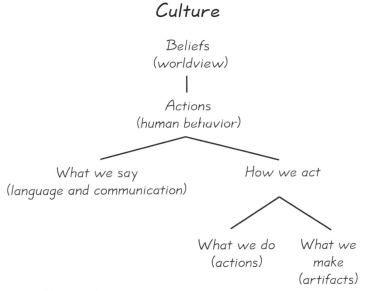

Culture

Beliefs
(worldview)

|

Actions
(human behavior)

What we say
(language and communication)

How we act

What we do
(actions)

What we
make
(artifacts)

Categories

"It also helps to understand culture when we understand some of the different categories of culture. One is geographical. Thus we speak of western culture, eastern culture, North American culture, urban and suburban culture. Another category is philosophical, such as modern culture and the postmodern culture. A third category is institutional, so a business, church, or school all have their own culture."

"So you're saying that every part of our life makes up our individual culture?" Bob was trying to clarify it in his mind.

"Yes, I believe so. Of course, some *parts* of your life will have more influence than others. For example, your ethnic origin may have more impact than the business you work in."

What Culture Isn't

Bob nodded and Steve leaned back in his chair and cleared his throat. "I'm aware of some misconceptions that Christians and churched people hold about culture," he said. "The most common misconception is that culture is inherently evil. I've noted that whenever Christian people—especially some on television and radio—mention culture, it's often in a negative context. This represents a misunderstanding of what the Scriptures teach about culture. What we must realize is that culture was an intrinsic part of the lives of Adam and Eve before the fall. They thought and acted while living in the Garden of Eden. Since God created Adam and Eve as thinking and acting persons and created the Garden of Eden, he, in effect, created culture. In addition, Genesis 1:31 says that, 'God saw all that he had made, and it was very good.' Thus God created culture and it was very good.

"Not only did Adam and Eve think and act, it's obvious that the Godhead does the same. For example, in Genesis 1 the Godhead's creative acts were the result of their creative thought and planning. If this is the case, and I think that it's obvious, then the Godhead relates and operates in a cultural context.

"Furthermore, the evidence seems to indicate that culture will be an intrinsic part of our future state in heaven. For instance, Revelation 7:9–10 reveals that people's cultural distinctives will be preserved, such as their ethnicity and language. We see much the same later in chapters 20 through 22 of Revelation, specifically Revelation 21:26."

"Does that mean, then, that culture is always good?" Bob asked.

"No, culture can be good or bad. We see a very different culture after the fall. In essence, culture was devastated by the fall. Sin pervaded everything including culture.

"We tend to view culture as an end in itself. It's not an end but a means or vehicle to an end. Paul indicates this in Romans 14:14 when he refers to food—a vital aspect of culture—as not unclean in itself. However, if someone regards a particular food as unclean, then for him or her it's unclean. Therefore, as a means to an end, culture can be used for good or bad. Another example is language. In James 3:9–12 James distinguishes two uses of the tongue, or language. On the one hand, people use it for good, such as praising God. On the other hand, people may use it to curse others who've been created in God's image. A hunter can use a gun to provide food for his family, while a criminal may use it to rob a store. The same scalpel can correct a baby's malfunctioning heart valve or take a baby's life by abortion."

Our Response to Culture

"So what should a Christian's response be to culture?" Bob asked.

"That's an important question for a pastor to ask, since each of us gives leadership to a church that has its own unique corporate culture. Christians tend to respond in one of three ways. They isolate themselves from culture, they accomodate themselves to it, or they minister within a specific cultural context."

Steve paused and drained his cup of coffee.

"You are going to explain those three responses, aren't you?" Bob asked.

Steve laughed. "Yes, of course. I just can't resist these donuts!" He took another one.

Isolation

"Okay, isolation represents one extreme. It argues that the Christian's proper response to culture is to separate from it. Isolationists believe that the culture is inherently evil and an enemy of the gospel. Many would equate it with the term *world* in the Bible and believe that John is warning us to avoid the world in such passages as John 12:31; 16:11; and 1 John 4:4 and 5:19. Supposedly Paul is doing the same in 2 Corinthians 4:4 and Ephesians 2:2. Separation from the world is first-degree separation. Some argue for second-degree separation as well. This view of isolation teaches that we must separate not only from the world but from anyone in Christianity that we feel may have compromised the gospel by embracing the world."

"Goodness! That is radical," Bob said. "How do you respond to people who hold such extreme views?"

"I respond to isolationists in several ways. First, the New Testament does use the term *world* for our culture. However, that usage describes culture when it's under the control of Satan, his forces, or men who pursue evil, not good. Isolationists totally miss the biblical teaching on culture as a means or vehicle for good or bad."

Bob looked confused and then his face brightened. "Oh, you mean the teachings about food and language."

"Yes," Steve said. "I wonder how isolationists explain Christ's incarnation when he came into this world, became a man, and embraced the good aspects of the culture? Isolationists tend to view culture as something 'out there'—an evil force beyond us that we can separate from. However, while culture is 'out there' it's also 'in here,'" Steve pointed at his head. "Not only is culture all around us, it's part of us. The language we speak and the thoughts we think are all part of our culture. Our ethnicity is a cultural distinctive. This presents a major dilemma for isolationists. How can you separate from that which is an intrinsic part of you, who you are?"

Accommodation

"Accommodation is the other extreme. It involves the Christian's accommodation or adoption of the extrinsic culture. Two forms exist. The first is the form held by liberalism. It believes that much of the culture of the fallen world is a friend of the gospel and argues that we must adopt the views of modern science, sociology, philosophy, and theology. These views include the acceptance of concepts such as radical feminism, homosexuality, and abortion, but would exclude biblical orthodoxy. Liberals advocate embracing the sinful use of the culture. Thus they conform to culture and buy into the spirit of the age. The problem with this view is that while leaning over to speak to the world, there's a danger you might fall in. And I believe most liberals have.

"Then there is a conservative form of accommodation. I'm surprised at the number of Christians who embrace or come very close to embracing this view. It argues that God endorses a particular culture or subculture as distinctly Christian. For some it's the first-century culture. Those, for example, who embrace patternism—we should follow the patterns of the first-century churches—tend to favor this view. These patterns, such as the church's possible meeting on the first day of the week and the use of wine in communion, were very much a part of the first-century culture.

"Others believe our twenty-first-century European or North American culture is endorsed by God. Unconsciously, if not consciously, we communicate to converts that our way of doing things (walking, talking, eating, greeting, and especially 'doing church') is better than and more Christian than theirs. A common example is when we send the message to unchurched lost people that they have to behave like churched people to be accepted. Many of them view churched people much like Dana Carvey's imitation of the 'church lady' on *Saturday Night Live* in the 1990s. They don't want any part of that."

"I have a number of people in my church," Bob interrupted, "who hold that view. Because some lost, unchurched visitors don't behave like them at church—they dress too casually, get up and go out of the service several times, and chew gum—they think there's something wrong with them."

Steve shook his head, "The message we send to them is that they must become like us and embrace our culture to be saved.

"The gospel, however, doesn't presuppose that any culture is superior to another."

"That's true," Bob said. "The middle-eastern culture our Lord lived in is very different from North American culture."

"Exactly!" Steve agreed. "While some cultures are more advanced than others, the gospel views them not as superior or inferior but as different. We don't have to embrace a culture along with the gospel to be saved. The church determined at the Jerusalem Council in Acts 15 that a Gentile doesn't have to become a Jew (be circumcised) to be saved! Neither was the first century superior to the twenty-first century. The fact that much of the New Testament was written in the first century and the church grew and developed at that time doesn't mean that God favored that culture any more than any other culture."

Contextualization

"The third possibility and the best response to culture is contextualization. Contextualization attempts to plant or reestablish churches and communicate the gospel in language and practices that are within people's cultural context so that the message makes sense and permits them to follow Christ. Therefore, it views culture as a means or vehicle that God, man, or Satan can use for their own purposes, whether good or evil. It teaches that a convert doesn't have to adopt or embrace another so-called Christian or church culture to be accepted or saved or to join a church. It uses indigenous cultural forms and practices to communicate biblical truth; otherwise, the gospel makes no sense.

"Though God is above and beyond human culture, he has chosen to work through man's culture and even, at times, to limit himself to that culture. For example, he chose to speak to men such as Adam, Moses, the prophets, and many others through human language.

Had he used some heavenly language, as mentioned in 1 Corinthians 13:1, they wouldn't have understood him.

"Jesus' incarnation is a great example of contextualization. He incarnated himself in a human body, learned a language, and lived among and learned from men. One reason he did this was to reveal himself to mankind in a way that made sense and communicated to them.

"Finally, Paul chose, rather than impose his own culture on those to whom he ministered, to adapt to them and the morally acceptable elements of their culture. Let's look at 1 Corinthians 9:19–22." Steve read, "'Though I am free and belong to no man, I make myself a slave to everyone, to win as many as possible. To the Jews I became like a Jew, to win the Jews. To those under the law I became like one under the law (though I myself am not under the law), so as to win those under the law. To those not having the law I became like one not having the law (though I am not free from God's law but am under Christ's law), so as to win those not having the law. . . . I have become all things to all men so that by all possible means I might save some.'"

Culture and the Gospel

"Okay, I see that. I think I understand what Paul is saying. But what is the relationship between the gospel and culture? Is it above or part of the culture?" Bob wanted to know.

"The gospel is supracultural in its origin and essence, but cultural in its interpretation and application. God, who transcends man's culture and is thus supracultural, is the source of the gospel. However, Christians originally recorded and communicated the gospel in the context of the the Greco-Roman culture. Today we interpret, study, and apply the gospel in the context of some culture, such as North American, European, Asian. Therefore, we must understand that though supracultural in function, the gospel will and should always exist in some cultural context. No supracultural form of the gospel exists.

"It's imperative that Christians and churches distinguish between the gospel and their culture. Failure to make this distinction mixes the two together in people's minds. For example, in a traditional mindset, mixing them communicates that acceptance of the gospel also includes the acceptance of certain cultural practices, such as singing the great hymns of the faith played on a piano or organ; wearing formal clothing such as coats, ties, and long dresses; or even, for women, wearing a head covering. And the same is true of a contemporary cultural mindset as well.

"We must discover how to use our culture and that of others to best clarify and promote the gospel. When we put the gospel into other people's cultural forms, whether North American or some other, we make it possible for them to understand it, embrace it, and communicate it to others. We seek to express the gospel in ways and forms that our target group— unchurched, lost North Americans, lost Asians, lost Javanese, and others—can understand. We must be sure that the forms we use carry meanings that convey the proper message. For example, in some contexts the use of wine as a part of communion could convey a negative message.

"Does that answer your question?" Steve asked.

"Yes, I think so," Bob said as he read his notes aloud:

Culture and the Gospel

- *The gospel is supracultural in its origin and essence, but cultural in its interpretation and application.*
- *It's imperative that Christians and churches distinguish between the gospel and their culture.*
- *We must discover how to use our culture and that of others to best clarify and promote the gospel.*

Culture and the Church

"A proper understanding of culture, the gospel, and the Scriptures teaches us much about 'doing church.' And the church in North America must take the lessons seriously if we are to accomplish Christ's mission. I want to mention several of these lessons," Steve said.

Culture Affects All Churches

"First, culture affects all churches. There are no exceptions. The question, therefore, isn't, Does culture affect what we do as a church? Rather the question is, Which culture primarily affects what we do as a church? Most older, established white churches in North America still reflect a western European culture. As I said before, their practices and customs were 'made in Europe.' Actually, Christian churches are among the few institutional vestiges of European culture that are still standing in America. Cultural practices such as the use of organ music, hymns, altars, pews, collection plates, kneelers, stained glass windows, a distinct architecture are western European, not biblical, in origin."

Bob chuckled. "That's true, but how many people stop to realize it?"

"Much the same is true of the new-paradigm churches that have rejected European culture in churches. Instead, they have adopted different cultural practices that are American, not biblical, in origin. So they're churches that are 'made in America.'"

Bob chuckled again.

"This is not necessarily bad," Steve said. "Remember that culture is a means that can be used for good or bad. If the people in our churches cling to a European culture and refuse to adjust when the culture all around them is changing, then it could be bad. When the culture, not the message, unnecessarily or unintentionally turns people off to the gospel and Christianity because it is out of touch, then it is bad. Unfortunately, far too many of our churches have consciously and unconsciously done this at the end of the twentieth century and the beginning of the twenty-first century. Unchurched people visit a church only to find that it is a culturally alienating experience—they don't understand the jargon ('temple talk'), can't relate to the music, and feel uncomfortable and out of place. Thus they wrongfully conclude that Christianity and the gospel are not for them when it's really the culture that turned them off. Add to this the practice in some churches that requires lost people to behave like churched people before the church will accept them."

"That's a big part of what Acts 15 was about," Bob added.

"That's right," Steve agreed.

Culture Affects Our Churches More Than We Realize

"Culture affects our churches more than we realize. I'm convinced that as much as 80 to 90 percent of what we do in our churches is culturally, not biblically, directed."

"Boy, that's amazing but you're probably right."

Steve continued, "An example is music. It plays a far greater role than most people realize, not only in the lives of our adults but in the lives of our young people. Musicians and their music exert a profound influence on today's youth culture. To ignore this or not be aware of it in our churches is to risk the alienation and loss of our youth to the cause of Christ. People in our churches have got to realize that today's traditional music was yesterday's contemporary music, and today's contemporary music is tomorrow's traditional music. For an older generation to impose their tastes on the new generation—no matter how innocently—means that both groups suffer in the long term. Those in the church must let the newer generations develop styles and a culture that best convey Christianity to them."

"This is hitting very close to home," Bob said. "One of my deacons once said, 'If the organ was good enough for Paul, then it's good enough for us!'"

"The problem is that most pastors and congregations aren't aware of the need to be culturally relevant. They believe, like your deacon, that if they change something, they're violating Scripture. For others, unfortunately, power is the issue. Regardless, the good news is that each church has a lot to say regarding its culture and it can choose to change."

Our Church Cultures Will Exclude Some People

"A third lesson is that our church cultures will exclude some people. Most of us desire to reach everyone, and that's good. However, a church that attempts to reach everyone in general will reach no one in particular. Once your church's culture is set, you'll exclude some people. It can't be helped. Some simply will not care for your church's style of music and so on. In effect, they're rejecting you. My point is that it's okay not to reach everybody. That's why so many different kinds of churches exist. It takes all kinds of churches to reach all kinds of people. The important thing is that we're *willing* to reach everyone and that we don't intentionally turn people off to the gospel.

"Now the question becomes, Who will we reach? The answer is those who are attracted to us and our culture. Those, for example, who like our style of worship. While there will be some exceptions, this is the norm. Therefore those who are attracted to us will form our target group. Just as Paul targeted the Gentiles and Peter targeted the Jews, we'll have a target group as well."

No Culture Is Superior

"I want to comment again on the fact that no culture is distinctly Christian and thus superior to another. God hasn't endorsed any culture as uniquely Christian. The Bible in no way encourages us to strive to be like the first century or any other century. This is one of the lessons we have to learn.

"Some knowingly or unknowingly package their particular culture with the gospel. On close examination, it's evident that the package is strangely western or denominational or may smack of capitalistic, middle-class American values. Though some of these values are good, we must be careful to distinguish between a Christian use of culture and labeling a culture as Christian."

The Church Should Remain Relevant to the Culture

"The church that exegetes the culture as well as the Scriptures should remain relevant to that culture."

Bob looked puzzled. "What do you mean?"

"Well, like the men of Issachar in 1 Chronicles 12:32, we should understand our times so that we know what to do to reach people. To exegete our culture helps us understand it—to discern what is good and bad about it and how to minister well to those who are a part of it."

"How do you do that?" Bob interrupted.

"I follow five steps," Steve said. "First, I build friendships with lost people. I've found that they won't seek me out; I have to seek them out, much as the Savior did, according to Luke 19:10. I invite my lost next-door neighbor to go jog around the park with me or play some basketball. I watch football with another lost friend.

"The second step is to try to listen well when people talk to me. That way I gain insight into who they are— their interests, their struggles, and their openness to spiritual things."

As Steve talked, Bob was making a list of the steps. He wrote a 3 on his pad and waited for Steve to go on.

"Third step: I try to read a lot. When most people are watching television, I'm reading the newspaper, magazines, and books. I want to know what my neighbors are reading and the ideas that they're exposed to. Fourth, I collect demographic information—general information about where people live, their education, marital status, and so on. And I collect psychographic information—what people value and how it influences their lifestyle. This information tells me much about our culture. Finally, on occasion, I'll conduct a community survey and ask people such questions as: Are you currently attending a church? What do you think is the greatest need in the community? Why don't more people attend church? What should churches do to reach people?"

"Wow, that's challenging!" Bob said. "I know I need to start doing some cultural exegesis." And he began to study his notes. He had listed the lessons Steve said the North American church must learn about culture.

The Culture and the Church

1. Culture affects all churches.
2. Culture affects our churches more than we realize.
3. Our church cultures will inevitably exclude some people.
4. No culture is distinctly Christian and superior to all the rest.
5. The church that exegetes the culture should remain relevant to that culture.

Then he had listed Steve's steps in exegeting the culture.

How to Exegete Your Culture

1. Build relationships with lost people.
2. Listen well to lost people.
3. READ, READ, READ.
4. Collect demographic and psychographic information.
5. Conduct a neighborhood survey.

Steve closed his Bible and leaned back in his chair. "Well, that's my theology of culture. I hope I didn't cover it so fast that you got lost."

"No!" Bob assured him. "I've got it all down." He patted his notepad. "I have a lot to study and put into practice over the summer. Hopefully, when we get together in the fall, I will have made some progress."

"I have no doubt about that," Steve said as the two men stood together. After prayer, Steve said, "Hey, man, thanks for the donuts!"

"Oh," Bob said, "here's something else for you." Bob handed Steve a bright red envelope.

"What's this?"

"It's just something to say thank you for spending all this time with me."

"This is great," Steve said, pulling the card out of the envelope. "A gift certificate to my favorite restaurant! How did you know?"

"Well, it's the best Italian restaurant in town, so I figured I couldn't go wrong. I hope you enjoy it."

"Thanks, Bob. These have been good times for me too. I'll look forward to starting again in the fall."

> For Scripture relating to what happened to culture because of the fall, see Genesis 3:14–19; 6:5.
>
> For Scripture teaching that God is the source of the gospel, see Galatians 1:11–12; 2 Timothy 3:16.

Appendix A
Core Values Audit

What are the core values of this ministry organization? Rate each of the core values listed below from 1 to 5 (1 being the lowest and 5 the highest). You need not be overly analytical. Work your way through the list quickly, going with your first impression.

_____ 1. godly leadership

_____ 2. a well-mobilized laity

_____ 3. Bible-centered preaching/teaching

_____ 4. the poor and disenfranchised

_____ 5. creativity and innovation

_____ 6. world missions

_____ 7. people

_____ 8. attractive grounds and facilities

_____ 9. financially responsible

_____ 10. the status quo

_____ 11. visitors

_____ 12. cultural relevance

_____ 13. prayer

_____ 14. sustained excellence/quality

_____ 15. fellowship/community

_____ 16. evangelism

_____ 17. family

_____ 18. God's grace

_____ 19. praise and worship

_____ 20. a Christian self-image

_____ 21. social justice

_____ 22. commitment

_____ 23. giving/tithing

_____ 24. counseling

_____ 25. civil rights

_____ 26. Christian education (all ages)

_____ 27. ordinances

_____ 28. equal rights

_____ 29. compassion

_____ 30. growth

_____ 31. community service

_____ 32. the environment

_____ 33. responsibility

_____ 34. the lordship of Christ

_____ 35. dignity

_____ 36. loyalty

_____ 37. fairness and equity

_____ 38. technology

_____ 39. efficiency

_____ 40. ethnic diversity

_____ 41. enthusiasm

_____ 42. discipline

_____ 43. teamwork

_____ 44. life (prolife)

_____ 45. authenticity

_____ 46. life-change

_____ 47. the Great Commission

_____ 48. humor

_____ 49. optimism

_____ 50. flexibility

_____ 51. other _____

_____

_____

Write down all the core values that received a rating of 4 or 5 (list no more than what you believe are the 12 most important values). Rank these according to priority (place the number 1 in front of the highest, 2 in front of the next highest, and so on).

Appendix B
Core Values Statement
Northpoint Community Church

The following presents the core values of Northpoint Community Church. We desire that they define and drive this ministry in the context of a warm and caring environment.

Christ's Headship

We acknowledge Christ as the head of our church and submit ourselves and all our activities to his will and good pleasure (Eph. 1:22–23).

Biblical Teaching

We strive to teach God's Word with integrity and authority so that seekers find Christ and believers mature in him (2 Tim. 3:16).

Authentic Worship

We desire to acknowledge God's supreme value and worth in our personal lives and in the corporate worship of our church (Rom. 12:1–2).

Prayer

We rely on private and corporate prayer in the conception, planning, and execution of all the ministries and activities of this church (Matt. 7:7–11).

Sense of Community

We ask all our people to commit to and fully participate in biblically functioning small groups where they may reach the lost, exercise their gifts, be shepherded, and thus grow in Christlikeness (Acts 2:44–46).

Family

We support the spiritual nurture of the family as one of God's dynamic means to perpetuate the Christian faith (2 Tim. 1:5).

Grace-Orientation

We encourage our people to serve Christ from hearts of love and gratitude rather than guilt and condemnation (Rom. 6:14).

Creativity and Innovation

We will constantly evaluate our forms and methods, seeking cultural relevance and maximum ministry effectiveness for Christ (1 Chron. 12:32).

Mobilized Congregation

We seek to equip all our uniquely designed and gifted people to effectively accomplish the work of our ministry (Eph. 4:11–13).*

Lost People

We value unchurched, lost people and will use every available Christ-honoring means to pursue, win, and disciple them (Luke 19:10).*

Ministry Excellence

Since God gave his best (the Savior), we seek to honor him by maintaining a high standard of excellence in all our ministries and activities (Col. 3:23–24).*

*These are aspirational values. While they are not yet our values, we are working hard at making them our core values.

Appendix C

Vision Statement
Northpoint Community Church

Vision is not about reality or what is. Vision is all about our dreams and aspirations or what could be.

At Northpoint Community Church, we envision our sharing the good news of Christ's death and resurrection with thousands of unchurched friends and people in our community, many of whom accept him as Savior.

We envision developing all our people—new believers as well as established believers—into fully functioning followers of Christ through people-friendly worship services, Sunday school, special events, and, most important, small groups.

We envision becoming a church of small groups where our people model biblical community: a safe place where we accept one another and are accepted, love and are loved, shepherd and are shepherded, encourage and are encouraged, forgive and are forgiven, and serve and are served.

We envision helping all our people—youth as well as adults—to discover their divine design so that they are equipped to serve Christ effectively in some ministry either within or outside our church. Our goal is that every member be a minister.

We envision welcoming numerous members into our body who are excited about Christ, experience healing in their family relationships and marriages, and grow together in love.

We envision recruiting, training, and sending out many of our members as missionaries, church planters, and church workers all over the world. We also see a number of our people pursuing short-term missions service in various countries. We envision planting a church in America or abroad every two years.

We envision a larger facility that will accommodate our growth and be accessible to the entire community. This facility will provide ample room for Sunday school, small groups, Bible study, prayer, and other meetings. While we do not believe that "bigger is better," numerical growth is a by-product of effective evangelism. Thus we desire to grow as God prospers us and uses us to reach a lost and dying world.

This is our dream—our vision of what could be!

Select Bibliography

Chapter 1
Pastors and Their Character

Kouzes, James M., and Barry Z. Posner. *Credibility.* San Francisco: Jossey-Bass, 1993.

Malphurs, Aubrey. *Maximizing Your Effectiveness.* Grand Rapids: Baker, 1995.

McIntosh, Gary, and Samuel D. Rima Sr. *Overcoming the Dark Side of Leadership: The Paradox of Personal Dysfunction.* Grand Rapids: Baker, 1998.

Ryrie, Charles C. *Balancing the Christian Life.* Chicago: Moody, 1969.

Sanders, J. Oswald. *Spiritual Leadership.* Chicago: Moody, 1980.

Swindoll, Charles R. *Integrity.* Grand Rapids: Zondervan, 1981.

Wiersbe, Warren W., and David W. Wiersbe, *Ten Power Principles for Christian Service: Ministry Dynamics for a New Century.* Grand Rapids: Baker, 1997.

Chapter 2
Pastors and Their Leadership

Gangel, Kenneth O. *Feeding and Leading.* Wheaton: Victor, 1989.

Jones, Bruce W. *Ministerial Leadership in a Managerial World.* Wheaton: Tyndale, 1988.

Kouzes, James M., and Barry Z. Posner. *Credibility.* San Francisco: Jossey-Bass, 1993.

Saucy, Robert L. *The Church in God's Program.* Chicago: Moody, 1972.

Chapter 3
Pastors and Their Churches

Barna, George. *The Power of Vision.* Ventura, Calif.: Gospel Light, 1992.

Frazee, Randy, with Lyle E. Schaller. *The Comeback Congregation.* Nashville: Abingdon, 1995.

Malphurs, Aubrey. *Advanced Strategic Planning.* Grand Rapids: Baker, 1999.

———. *Developing a Dynamic Mission for Your Ministry.* Grand Rapids: Kregel, 1998.

———. *Developing a Vision for Your Ministry in the 21st Century,* 2d ed. Grand Rapids: Baker, 1999.

———. *The Ministry Nuts and Bolts: What They Don't Teach Pastors in Seminary.* Grand Rapids: Kregel, 1998.

———. *Strategy 2000.* Grand Rapids: Kregel, 1997.

———. *Values-Driven Leadership.* Grand Rapids: Baker, 1996.

Chapter 4
Pastors and Their People

Belasco, James A., and Ralph C. Stayer. *Flight of the Buffalo.* New York: Warner Books, 1993.

Dethmer, Jim. "Moving in the Right Circles." *Leadership* (fall 1992): 86–91.

Reed, Bobbie, and John Westfall, *Building Strong People: How to Lead Effectively*. Grand Rapids: Baker, 1997.

Saucy, Robert L. *The Church in God's Program*. Chicago: Moody, 1972.

Chapter 5
Pastors and Change

Getz, Gene A. *Sharpening the Focus of the Church*. Chicago: Moody, 1974.

Hull, Bill, *7 Steps to Transform Your Church*. Grand Rapids: Revell, 1997.

Malphurs, Aubrey. *Doing Church: A Biblical Guide for Leading Ministries through Change*. Grand Rapids: Kregel, 1999.

———. *Pouring New Wine into Old Wineskins*. Grand Rapids: Baker, 1993.

Schaeffer, Francis A. *The Church at the End of the Twentieth Century*. Wheaton: Crossway, 1970.

White, James Emery. *Rethinking the Church: A Challenge to Creative Redesign in an Age of Transition*. Grand Rapids: Baker, 1997.

Chapter 6
Pastors and Culture

Frame, John M. *Contemporary Worship Music*. Phillipsburg, N.J.: P & R Publishing, 1997.

Getz, Gene. *Sharpening the Focus of the Church*. Chicago: Moody, 1974.

Index

Conspiracy of Kindness (Sjogren), 112
contextualization, 133–34
core concepts, 58
core values. *See* values
core values audit, 65, 143–45
corporation, church as, 86–89
Credibility (Kouzes and Posner), 55
culture: accommodation to, 131–33; categories of, 127–28; church and, 136–41; contextualization and, 133–34; definition of, 125–28; exegesis of, 140–41; forms and, 108; gospel and, 134–36; importance of, 122–25; influence of, 122, 137–38; isolation from, 130–31; misconceptions of, 128–29; responses to, 129–34; theology of, 121–22

devotions, 31–32, 36
disciple, 72, 77
Doing Church: A Biblical Guide for Leading Ministries through Change (Malphurs), 119

elders: leadership of, 49–51; miscellaneous functions of, 53; as pastors, 41; plurality of, 41–42, 44–45; protection by, 51–52; qualifications for, 45–46, 50; teaching and, 52–53. *See also* bishops; pastors
evaluation, 32
evangelism, 57, 101, 102, 112–13
excitement, 85–86

false teachers, 51
Flight of the Buffalo (Belasco and Stayer), 97
forms: basis for, 108; characteristics of, 107–8; definition of, 106–11; discovery of, 116–17; evangelistic, 112–13; implication of, 109; organizational, 113–14; purpose of, 110–11; usage of, 109
freedom: implications of, 117; limitations on, 117–18; restrictions on, 118
fruit of the Spirit, 25–26
functions: basis of, 102–3; characteristics of, 101–2; definition of, 101–4; discovery of, 105–6; evaluation of, 103; examples of, 104–5; implication of, 103; purpose of, 104; usage of, 103

gifts, spiritual, 21–22
godly character: conflict with ministry, 21–24; essence of, 25–26; need for, 19–21. *See also* character
gospel, 134–36
Graham, Billy, 112
Great Commission, 68, 72, 84, 94
Greek-English Lexicon of the New Testament and Other Early Christian Literature (Bauer), 55

heart, 27
hermeneutics, 119
Holy Spirit, fruit of, 25–26
hypocrisy, 22–24

Aubrey Malphurs is the president of Vision Ministries International and is available for training and consulting on various topics related to leadership, vision, divine design, church planting, and church renewal, as well as a number of other topics. Those wishing to use his services may contact him at:

Dallas Theological Seminary
3909 Swiss Avenue
Dallas, TX 75204
214-841-3777
fax: 214-841-3697
e-mail: Aubrey_Malphurs@dts.edu